Contents

The
Chinchilla
Handbook

Sharon L. Vanderlip, DVM

Filled with Full-color Photographs
Illustrations by Michele Earle-Bridges

BARRON'S

Acknowledgment

I would like to thank my husband, Jack Vanderlip, DVM, for his help as an expert veterinary consultant and for critically reviewing the final manuscript. Special thanks are due to David B. Hyde, DVM, for a thorough evaluation and helpful suggestions, and to my wonderful editor, Pat Hunter. Thanks to my husband and our daughter, Jacquelynn Vanderlip, for keeping the house in order, caring for our animals, and doing all the things I left undone so I could take time to write. Without their enormous help, this manuscript would still be a work in progress!

All inquiries should be addressed to:
Barron's Educational Series, Inc.
250 Wireless Boulevard
Hauppauge, New York 11788
www.barronseduc.com

ISBN-13: 978-0-7641-3266-7
ISBN-10: 0-7641-3266-0

Library of Congress Catalog Card No. 2005053030

Library of Congress Cataloging-in-Publication Data
Vanderlip, Sharon Lynn.
    The chinchilla handbook / Sharon Vanderlip ; illustrations by Michele Earle-Bridges.
        p. cm.
    Includes bibliographical references and index.
    ISBN-13: 978-0-7641-3266-7
    ISBN-10: 0-7641-3266-0
    1. Chinchillas as pets. I. Earle-Bridges, Michele. II. Title.

SF459.C48V36   2006
636.9′3593—dc22   2005053030

Printed in China
9 8

About the Author

Sharon Vanderlip, DVM, has provided veterinary care to exotic and domestic animal species for more than 25 years. She has written numerous books and articles in scientific and general publications. Dr. Vanderlip served as clinical veterinarian for the University of California at San Diego School of Medicine, has worked on collaborative projects with the Zoological Society of San Diego, and has owned her own veterinary practice. She is former chief of veterinary services for the National Aeronautics and Space Administration (NASA) and is a consultant for wildlife projects. Dr. Vanderlip has won awards for her writing and dedication to animal health. She has owned and loved chinchillas and can be contacted for seminars at *www.SharonVanderlip.com*

Photo Credits

Gerry Bucsis and Barbara Somerville: pages vi, 4, 6, 7, 8, 9, 11, 13, 15, 16, 18, 19, 21, 23, 24, 29, 32, 35, 36, 39, 40, 41, 42, 45, 46, 48, 49, 50, 51, 55, 56, 57, 58, 59, 60, 66, 68, 76, 78, 79, 88, 89, 90, 93, 106, 109, 114, 118, 119 (both), 120, 124, 127, 134, 135, 141, 142, 144, 145, 146, 147, 148 (both), 149, 153; Isabelle Francais: pages 25, 33, 63, 65, 71, 74, 100, 101, 107, 112, 122, 125, 130, 138, 151

Cover Photos

Gerry Bucsis and Barbara Somerville

Important Note

This pet handbook tells the reader how to buy and care for chinchillas. The advice given in the book applies to healthy animals with good dispositions obtained from a reputable source. Extraordinary efforts have been made to ensure the treatment recommendations are precise and in agreement with standards accepted at the time of publication. If your chinchilla shows any signs of illness, you should consult a veterinarian immediately since some diseases are dangerous for humans. If you have any questions about an illness, or if you have been bitten by your chinchilla, consult a physician immediately. Some people are allergic to animal hair, dander, saliva, urine, and feces or they have a weakened immune system and cannot be exposed to animals. If you are not sure, consult your physician before you acquire a chinchilla.

Be sure to instruct children in the safe handling of chinchillas and supervise children when they are handling chinchillas. Never leave your pets or small children alone with chinchillas.

Chapter One
The Charming Chinchilla

The chinchilla is a rare gift of nature—a gentle animal with large ears, bright eyes, and a soft, luxurious coat. Its exquisite beauty is surpassed only by its mystery and charm. The chinchilla's incredible story, from aeons past up to the present day, sparks the imagination. From the time of its discovery, the chinchilla has intrigued humans. Chinchillas were used for food and fur by the Indians of Chile, trapped and poached to near extinction for their plush pelts, exported worldwide for the fur industry, and studied in laboratory research. It is not surprising that along the way this attractive and versatile animal also captured the attention and hearts of animal lovers around the world—including *you*!

This book will give you the facts about the mystery, history, biology, and behavior of these wonderful animals. It will also clear up some misconceptions and misinformation. Best of all, this book will give you the information you need to take excellent care of your new pet—the

The standard gray chinchilla is well camouflaged in the lava rock terrain of the Andes Mountains.

world's most beautiful rodent—the chinchilla!

Chinchilla Names and Places

Chinchillas are as exotic as their name sounds, but where did such an unusual name originate? Quechuan languages were spoken in the Incan Empire and are spoken in the central Andes today. Experts think that the name *chinchilla* is a phoenetic rendering of the Quechuan words *chin*, meaning "silent," and *sinchi*, meaning "courageous" or "strong." This appears to be how the Chincha Indians earned their name. The Chincha Indians used chinchillas for food, fur, and pets (making them, perhaps, the world's first chinchilla pet owners!). It has been suggested that the word *chinchilla* was created by the Spaniards in the early 1500s when they encountered the Chincha Indians. According to this line of thought, the Spaniards called the animals chinchilla. The addition of the letters "lla" to *chin* and *sinchi* make the word diminutive and could be inter-

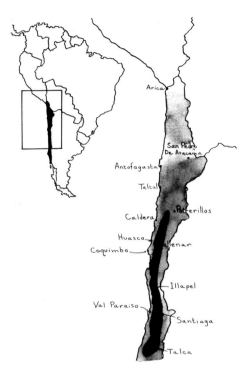

Centuries ago, chinchillas could be found in parts of Argentina, Bolivia, Chile, and Peru. Today, wild chinchillas are rare and their territories are restricted to the rugged Andes mountain of Chile.

preted to mean "little Chincha," named after the Chincha Indians. The word combination could also literally mean small, silent, strong, and courageous. These adjectives do not really describe the chinchilla precisely because chinchillas are not always silent, but more about that later!

The words *laniger* and *brevicaudata* are Latin words meaning "woolly" and "short tail," respectively. So the names for the two species of chinchilla in existence today, *Chinchilla laniger* and *Chin-*

chilla brevicaudata, are an interesting combination of Quechuan and Latin words, with a touch of Spanish ("lla") added.

In the 1700s, the scientific name for chinchillas was *Mus laniger*, but there was some disagreement about the animal that was being described and the accuracy of the description. *Lanigera* has also been used in place of *laniger*. However, the International Commission on Zoological Nomenclature requested that *Chinchilla laniger* be placed on the list of official scientific names.

Chinchillas originate from the rugged terrain of the Andes and north-central mountain chains of Chile. Hundreds of years ago, before their populations were decimated by fur trappers, chinchillas could be found in parts of Chile, Bolivia, Argentina, and Peru. Today they have a much smaller range and, sadly, are endangered. Even though chinchillas are now protected in the wild by law, their population continues to decline every year. The drop in animal numbers is attributed in part to their fragmented territories, caused by the burning and harvesting of the algarrobilla shrub, and also possibly due to competition with other rodent species in the region (degus and chinchilla rats) for resources. Some sources state that illegal trapping continues to be a problem.

Fortunately, chinchillas do well and reproduce in captivity. The vast majority of chinchillas in the United States are *C. laniger* (reportedly more than 99 percent). The majority of chinchillas maintained on protected ranches in Chile are *C. brevicaudata* (also reportedly more than 99 percent).

Unsolved Mystery

Some chinchilla books suggest that chinchillas evolved from large chinchilla-like animals called Megamys that existed aeons ago and were roughly the size of cattle. It is hard to imagine cattle-sized animals grazing in the barren, volcanic rock regions of the Andes, unless the region was very different at the time, had lush vegetation to support large herbivorous animals, and the animals were adapted for mountainous terrain. Chinchillas apparently never lived outside of the regions in which they lived at the time of their discovery, although we cannot be certain.

Because of the incomplete fossil record, the origin of hystricomorph rodents, such as the chinchilla, has been a topic of hot debate for decades. Lively discourse still continues among scientists as to the chinchilla's true origins. It is generally accepted that all South American rodents had a common ancestor somewhere, sometime—but where and when remain a mystery.

In the proceedings from the Zoological Society of London, authorities discuss not only what is known but also what remains to be discovered about chinchillas and other hystricomorph rodents. Many researchers are convinced the chinchilla's ancestors came from North America during

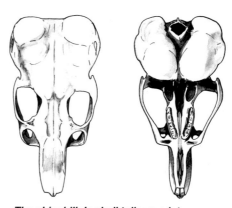

The chinchilla's skull tells us a lot about its evolution and ancestry and its relationship to other rodents.

the Eocene period (about 55 million years ago) and that they evolved separately from rodents in Africa that resembled them. Scientists base their idea on specific skull, jaw, and tooth development they believe rules out the likelihood of a direct descendant from an African species. They have also found fossils of possible ancestral rodents in Texas and Central America to support their theory.

Other scientists believe the chinchilla's ancestors evolved during the same time period but from a very primitive African mammal, which itself was derived from partly African and partly Eurasian predecessors. In the middle Eocene to lower Oligocene periods (about 40 million years ago), these very small animals would have crossed the Atlantic Ocean, presumably on rafts formed from wood, leaves, and debris carried by ocean currents. It may sound incredible, but this method of migration is not uncommon. Besides, according to plate tectonics (conti-

This dark ebony chinchilla is enjoying a tasty mulberry branch.

nental drift), continents were located closer together at that time. The cross–Atlantic Ocean voyage proposed to have taken place millions of years ago would have been approximately 1,800 miles (8,300 km)—much shorter than it is today, yet still quite a challenge for a group of small, ancestral rodents!

Researchers have discovered a worm that parasitizes rodents in both West Africa and South America. This parasite lends support to the raft migration theory, suggesting that when rodents crossed the oceans millions of years ago, they brought their specific parasites with them.

So what about the large Megamys? Where does it fit in? We hope to discover more fossils and more clues and to integrate new information with molecular studies. Until then, the chinchilla's intriguing secrets will continue to remain great mysteries.

Struggle for Survival

We may not know the chinchilla's story in the predawn era. However, we do know that from the time humans set foot in chinchilla territory in pre-Incan times, they valued chinchilla fur as a luxury. Historians tell us that the Incas used chinchilla skins and furs to make their blankets and that the Chincha Indians kept chinchillas for food, fur, and pets.

When the Spanish conquistador Francisco Pizarro captured and killed the Incan emperor Atahuallpa on

November 16, 1532, the course of history for South America and for chinchillas was changed forever. After the death of the Incan emperor, Spanish soldiers explored, invaded, and conquered the Incan empire—and Europeans discovered and exploited the chinchilla. Queen Isabella of Spain is credited with being the first European to sport a chinchilla coat. (Incidentally, more than 130 chinchilla pelts are used to make a full-length coat!)

By the late 1700s, chinchilla fur was being exported in significant quantities to Europe. As demand for chinchilla fur increased steadily, the number of pelts exported increased as well and millions of pelts were exported in the 1800s. Almost 500,000 pelts were shipped from Chile in 1899 alone. As a result, wild chinchillas were very rare indeed. It became apparent that without immediate action to protect the species, chinchillas would no longer exist. Unfortunately, even though the governments of Peru, Bolivia, Argentina, and Chile established laws protecting the animals, the dangerously low population and determined poachers continued to threaten the future of the species. In the 1920s, the South American governments took action by setting up some protected chinchilla farms, but it was too little, too late. The farms consisted almost exclusively of *C. brevicaudata* because *C. laniger* were no longer to be found. Strangely, an American mining engineer working for the Anaconda Copper Company in Chile managed to save *C. laniger*. If it were not for the extraordinary efforts of Mathias F. Chapman, you would not have your cuddly pet today.

From the Brink of Extinction

As is often the case in recording history, stories change as they are repeated over the years by different authors. Certainly the best sources of information are those closest to the situation and those who have direct knowledge of the historical events, such as eye witnesses or direct participants.

Chapman was an animal lover working in Chile when he was shown some chinchilla pelts. His dream was to bring chinchillas to the United States, save them from extinction, and raise them for fur. He reportedly enlisted the help of 23 trappers, and trapping efforts continued at altitudes of 10,400 feet (3,170 m) and higher, where the better-quality animals could be found. All of the chinchillas that were trapped (some historians give the total number to be 17) were *C. laniger*.

Accounts vary from this point. Most pet books state that the government would give permission for Chapman to export only 11 animals and that he selected three females and eight males. However, Parker, who was a close friend, employee, and associate of Chapman, states in his book that Chapman imported 12 chinchillas to the United States: three females and nine males. His book also shows photos of the permission form from the Chilean government

It is hard to imagine that all of our pet chinchillas, including this beautiful beige, are direct descendents of the original 13 chinchillas imported to the United States by Mathias Chapman.

for 12 chinchillas (and a cat!) and the United States Department of Agriculture letter of approval to import 12 chinchillas.

Another apparent misconception perpetuated by many sources is that Chapman had to bring the animals down from the mountains to the coastal seaport slowly, a hundred feet (30 m) at a time, so that they could acclimate to the difference in altitude. According to authorities Houston and Prestwich, as well as Parker, this story is false and the animals came down the mountain quickly by train from Potrerillos to the coast. They were then transported by the coastal steamer *Palena* to Callao, Peru, and then by the Japanese steamship freighter *Anyu Maru* to San Pedro, California, and docked on February 22, 1923.

Chapman went to great lengths to watch over his chinchillas and to keep them comfortable and cool during the long voyage. According to Parker, one chinchilla died on the trip and two were born, making a total of 13 chinchillas arriving in the United States on February 22, 1923. Once again, reports vary. Some books report that only one animal was born, others say only 11 animals arrived. However, the information supplied by Parker appears to be the most reliable. The veterinary literature also accepts that 13 chinchillas were originally imported and that all domestic chinchillas in the United States are descendants of the 13 individuals brought to the United States in 1923. With Chapman's importation and dedication, chinchilla ranching in America began!

After much hard work, Chapman successfully developed a small herd of 100 chinchillas. Unfortunately, several were stolen from him (reports vary again, from 32 animals to almost 50 animals stolen) and taken to Germany, where they reportedly died because they were not cared for properly. Despite these obstacles, Chapman managed to increase his herd over time. As a result, hundreds of chinchilla farms were established in the twentieth century. Some sources report that up until the 1950s, 10 to 50 chinchillas continued to be exported annually to the United States. (Detailed histories of chinchilla ranching, breeders, importation, colors, clubs, and shows are available through many sources listed under "Useful Addresses and Literature." Do not be surprised, though, if they do not all agree on their historical accounts, show rules, or color definitions!)

Since the mid-1800s, laboratories around the world have used chinchillas as research models, especially for studying ears and hearing. Although chinchillas are used much less in laboratories than other rodent species, they have done their fair share to contribute to and advance medical science and benefit human health.

Fortunately for today's chinchillas, not all are used for the fur industry or medical research. Many are loved for their companionship and beauty and hold a well-deserved place in our hearts as precious pets. It is amazing to think that our pet chinchillas are

Species Name	Country of Origin
Chinchilla laniger	Chile
Chinchilla brevicaudata	Chile

descendents of Chapman's traveling companions!

A Remarkable Rodent

Your pet belongs to a group of the most successful, diverse, and numerous of mammalian species: rodents. The words *rodent* and *rodentia* are derived from the Latin word *rodere*, which means "to gnaw." This refers to a rodent's need to chew on hard objects constantly to keep the teeth from growing too long. The most important character-

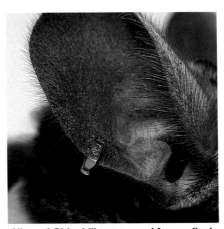

All ears! Chinchillas are used for medical research to study ears and hearing. Chinchilla breeders identify their animals with ear tags, such as the one on this dark ebony chinchilla.

Chinchilla teeth grow throughout life. Chew toys are necessary to prevent dental overgrowth and to keep the teeth chiseled and sharp.

istic shared by all rodents is the continual growth of their teeth throughout their entire lives. To understand your chin's personality, habits, instincts, and various requirements better, you should have an appreciation of what a rodent is.

Rodents are remarkably uniform in structural characters. They are grouped and classified according to anatomical characteristics, similarities in teeth and bone structure, origin, and lifestyle. All rodents have four incisors, two upper and two lower (the lower incisors are longer than the upper incisors). These front teeth grow throughout life, continuously being pushed up from the bottom of the jaw. This growth compensates for the constant wear on the teeth from biting hard objects and for abrasion between the upper and lower pairs that maintain a chisel-like sharpness. No nerves are in the front teeth, except at the base where they grow, and continual wear of the incisors maintains very sharp cutting surfaces.

Rodents do not have canine teeth or anterior premolars, so there is a rather large space, called the diastema, between the front teeth and the cheek teeth (premolars and molars). Like the incisors, the cheek teeth grow continuously throughout life. They are used for grinding (chinchillas grind and gnaw; they do not chew) and may have many peculiar patterns. These dental patterns, as well as jaw structure, are useful to zoologists and paleontologists for determining how different rodent species developed over time, their relationship to each other, and their origin.

You are, no doubt, already familiar with some more common rodents, such as rats, mice, and hamsters. Chinchillas not only look different, they *are* different! For example, they have special nutritional requirements, unique drug sensitivities, and specific behaviors. They have a much longer gestation period than most other rodent species. Gestation for a chinchilla is more than three months (105 to 118 days for *C. laniger* and as long as 128 days for *C. brevicaudata*), compared to 2½ to 3 weeks (16 to 21 days) for some other rodent species, such as hamsters and mice. Chinchilla babies (kits) are born with their eyes open and their teeth

Chinchilla pets in North America are of the species Chinchilla laniger.

erupted. They are fully furred and able to walk around within an hour of birth and ready to go! Rats, mice, and hamsters give birth to naked, helpless young whose eyes do not open for about two weeks (10 to 14 days). Your precious, *precocious* pet is no ordinary rodent!

The Chinchilla Family Tree

Animals, insects, and plants are classified and grouped according to their differences and similarities. Names are assigned according to kingdom, phylum, class, order, family, genus, and species. With each progressive category, animals grouped together are more closely related. For example, all animals are part of the Kingdom Animalia, but only rodents are members of the Order Rodentia.

Animals can be named according to a special characteristic of their group, named after the person who discovered them, or even named after the geographical area they naturally inhabit. As mentioned earlier, the chinchilla is named after Quechuan words from its country of origin plus Latin words describing its appearance.

The chinchilla is a member of the Kingdom Animalia (animal kingdom), the Phylum Chordata (animals having spinal columns), and the Class Mammalia. The word Mammalia refers to the mammary glands (mammae, teats, or breasts). Newborn and baby mammals are nourished by milk from their mothers' breasts. All warmblooded animals with hair or fur have mammary glands and belong to the Class Mammalia.

Within the Order Rodentia are three suborders. The chinchilla belongs to the Suborder Caviomorpha. As previously mentioned, caviomorph rodents are believed to be either descendents of African Phiomorpha, a group of animals that lived during the Oligocene period approximately 40 million years ago,

Mistaken Identity: The Costina Chinchilla

In the old literature, you will find reference to the costina chinchilla. The costina was considered by some to be a completely different species from *C. laniger* and *C. brevicaudata* because of its pointier nose; narrower, longer ears; slimmer, smaller body size; humped back; different coat quality (longer, shaggier fur over the hips), texture, and color (tendency to a tan and yellowish fur color and a noticeable sheen); and prolific reproductive ability. It was usually found at lower elevations and weighed between 8 and 11 ounces (226 to 311 grams).

The costina chinchilla was sometimes referred to as *C. lanigera bennett* or *C. lanigera costina* by those experts who recognized early on that the costina was actually *C. laniger* in disguise. Costina-type animals are probably the result of variations in body, coat, and reproduction influenced by regional differences (such as lower altitudes), environmental adaptations, or partial genetic isolation from other *C. laniger* when they lived in the wild. Detailed genetic studies will give us more answers. For now, though, a big part of the mystery is solved and we know what the costina really is!

or descendents of animals that evolved 55 million years ago in North America.

The Caviomorpha suborder is made up of 29 Recent rodent families. In paleozoological terms, the word *recent* refers to the Recent era, which corresponds to the end of the

last ice age, about 13,000 years ago. The chinchilla belongs to the Super-family Chinchilloidea, the Family Chinchillidae, and the Subfamily Chinchillinae. Families may be further divided into genera (plural for *genus*), a collection of even more closely related animals. There are at least 426 recognized rodent genera. There are only 3 genera in the Chinchillidae family: the genus *Chinchilla*, to which chinchillas belong, and the genera *Lagidium* and *Lagostomus*, to which the mountain viscacha and plains viscacha belong, respectively. This means that the viscachas are the chinchilla's closest living relatives.

In the past, there has been some variation in the way chinchillas were grouped and classified. Some people considered three subspecies of chinchillas to exist: *C. laniger*, *C. brevi-caudata*, and a chinchilla referred to as the costina.

The confusion was due mostly to the differences in appearance between the three animal "types." We now know that isolated popula-tions, natural selection, artificial selection, experimental breeding, line breeding, and inbreeding can all pro-duce animals with a variety of traits, such as body type, size, conforma-tion, head shape, coat quality, and color. Closely related (but different) species that inhabit similar environ-ments and that have evolved to adapt to them can share characteris-

Nature's Test

One of nature's tests of a true species is the animals' ability to inter-breed and reproduce successfully. If they can, they are members of the same species. Some animals can interbreed, but their offspring are hybrids and unable to reproduce. For example, horses and donkeys can interbreed, but their offspring, a mule or a hinny, is sterile and cannot repro-duce (except in a few very extraordi-nary cases).

A similar situation holds true for chinchillas. When *C. laniger* is crossed with *C. brevicaudata*, the gestation period is in between the normal gesta-tion period of either species and hybrid male offspring are infertile. Although the female offspring may be fertile, when they are bred (backcrossed to either species), about two-thirds of their offspring are sterile. In short, it is not a genetic match. According to nature's rules, the two types of chin-chillas are also two different species.

tics or resemble one another very closely. In the same way, identical species from isolated populations living in different areas may have more specifically adapted to their environments and differ from each other in their appearance. The costina is a good example. The truth is that the costina is actually a variation on a theme and is another body type of *C. laniger*.

It is reasonable to assume that the costina body and coat types are the result of genes not normally expressed or observed in *C. laniger* but obviously present in the *C. laniger* gene pool. How do we know that the costina is not a separate species from *C. laniger*? We know because it can successfully reproduce when bred to *C. laniger*. Different species do not interbreed and reproduce successfully. We also know from recent genetic studies conducted

in 2004 that only two species of chinchillas exist: *C. laniger* and *C. brevicaudata*.

As you study more about chinchillas, you may come across literature that refers to them as South American hystricognaths or hystricomorph rodents. Do not let this confuse you. The word *hystricomorph* has both systematic classification and structural meanings. Hystricomorph refers to a particular type of skull and muscle structure seen in certain rodent species and a very rare type of bottom jaw structure and angulation, called a hystricognathous mandible. These different zoological names simply reflect what scientists believe about the origins and evolution of the chinchilla, its ancestors, and its relatives throughout the ages.

Classification and Controversy

Chinchilla classification is not easy! If you think the nomenclature, taxonomy, and theories are complicated, you are right. Zoologists and paleontologists have taken countless years of study and research to sort through the scant evidence and paltry fossil record natural history has provided. In addition, experts do not always totally agree.

Now combine molecular biology with natural history and watch the sparks fly! A group of scientists studied some genetic material from various rodents and compared them. The researchers suggested that South American rodents are different enough from rats and mice that they

Chinchillas depend on their long whiskers to help them navigate through obstacles.

should be removed from the Order Rodentia. They believe that their findings should make scientists reconsider rodent classification and that the chinchilla and some of its relatives (including the guinea pig) should be assigned an order of their own.

On the other end of the spectrum sits the vast majority of scientists who maintain that the chinchilla is definitely a rodent until additional research proves otherwise. They admit that wide variation occurs among rodents and insist that studying the genetic material of only three animal species (out of more than 2,000 rodents in existence) is not enough to draw such all-encompassing conclusions. This group of scientists reminds us that

many anatomical features are specific to rodents, such as the bone structure and musculature of their entire head region, the teeth, and jaw musculature. Additional features characteristic of rodents are also not evident on the surface. For example, the fetal membranes found in rodents are unique among mammals, as well as their pattern of fetal development.

We have learned a lot about the chinchilla, but there is still so much to learn and each new discovery creates new questions. Yet, with all the uncertainty comes a greater appreciation for the history and mysteries surrounding our charming chinchilla companions! Until we have all the answers—and that will not be any time soon!—we can all agree on one

Chinchilla Weights and Measures

	C. laniger	C. brevicaudata
Adult male weight	Up to 21 ounces (600 g)	More than 24 ounces (680 g)
Adult female weight	Up to 28 ounces (800 g)	More than 24 ounces (680 g)
Adult Length	Approximately 10 inches (260 mm)	More than 12.5 inches (320 mm)
Ears	More rounded and longer, approximately 1.77 inches (more than 45 mm)	Shorter and less rounded, approximately 1.25 inches (less than 32 mm)
Head	Broad head, blunt nose	Broad head, blunt nose
Body conformation	Good conformation, more refined neck and shoulders	Larger, more robust and blockier body type, larger through neck and shoulders
Coat type	Long, dense, woolly	Long, dense, woolly
Tail	Longer, more than 5 inches (more than 130 mm)	Shorter, less than 4 inches (less than 100 mm)
Number of vertebrae in tail	23	20

thing: the shy, gentle, chinchilla is arguably the most beloved, interesting, and attractive rodent in existence today!

Chinchilla Characteristics

Weighing about 1 to 2 ounces (35 to 70 g) at birth and gaining a little more than a pound (600 to 800 g) by the time it is fully grown, a chinchilla requires both hands to hold it securely and comfortably. From the tip of its nose to the end of its rump, an adult measures 10 to 12 inches (26 to 32 cm) in length and has a 4- to 5-inch tail (10 to 13 cm) with coarse hair that ends in a tuft. C.

brevicaudata derives its name from the fact that it has a shorter tail than C. laniger.

The chinchilla's endearing appearance is partly attributable to its broad head, bright eyes, and rounded ears that give it an impish, yet soft and inquisitive expression. Long whiskers, or vibrissae, accentuate the broad face. The eyes are located on the sides of the head (instead of the front of the face) to allow a wider field of vision so it is easier to detect approaching predators.

Chinchillas have a compact body. The forelimbs are much shorter than the hind legs. The forefeet have five

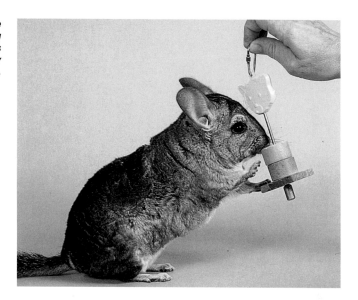

digits with very short claws. Unlike most animals, the tibia of the hind limbs is longer than the femur. The hind feet have three digits with short claws and one vestigial (rudimentary) digit with a very small claw.

The plush, soft coat consists of hair 1 to 2 inches (2 to 4 cm) in length, arranged in bands (usually gray, white, and black bands). Wool hairs grow in clusters around guard hairs. For every two clusters of wool hairs a single guard hair grows in the center. As many as 50 to 75 hairs or more can grow from a single skin pore, and this is what makes the coat so dense and plush.

Chinchilla coats come in a variety of colors and patterns. They shed, or slip, easily. Most chinchillas are gray, blue, or silver on the upper parts of their bodies, with yellow-white or light coloration on the under parts. Other colors range from white, beige, and tan to charcoal, black, and varying shades in between (see pages 143–145).

Chinchillas have very sensitive hearing and large auditory bullae. They are used in research to study ears and hearing. They also have a keen sense of smell.

Chinchillas are smart and easy to train. They are also smart enough to train *you*! They know what is needed to make their owners cater to their every desire. Just wait and see. Before you know it, you will be at your chin's beck and call, feeding treats and catering to it when it demands affection. You will be shopping for the perfect toys and trying to find a way to spend as much time as possible with your little companion. Chinchillas are bright, cuddly, and curious—so get ready to enjoy the cutest (and softest) pet you'll ever know!

Chapter Two

Is a Chinchilla the Right Pet for You?

From the time of their discovery hundreds of years ago to the time of their near extinction, chinchillas have been cherished for their plush, luxurious fur. Not until their relatively recent domestication, though, have chinchillas truly captured the hearts of animal lovers worldwide, who quickly recognized that this charming creature was more than a beautiful fur ball. The true value of the chinchilla is not one of money and pelts. The true value of the chinchilla for the naturalist, scientist, and pet owner is priceless. By studying chinchillas, we can learn a lot about natural history, biology, and behavior. There is no way to measure the enormous scientific value these charismatic critters offer us.

The chinchilla is a bright, attractive, inquisitive animal with a delightful personality. No wonder they have become lovable companions for so many people and continue to soar in popularity. The ultrasoft fur, attractive coat color variations, big bright eyes, and soft expression are just the icing on the cake that makes chinchillas all

Chinchillas vary as much in personality as they do in appearance.

the more appealing. Yes, the secret is out—chinchillas make wonderful pets! Who would not want to bring one home? However, chinchillas are not for everyone. So let us take a closer look at them so you will know if one (or more!) is the right pet for you.

An "Exotic" Pet

Chinchillas are sometimes referred to as "exotic pets," but what does that mean? An exotic pet is usually one that is not native, may live in the wild, and is not a common, everyday pet. Chinchillas, being recently domesticated and originating from South America, certainly fit the description. Although they are an unusual pet, they are no longer rare in captivity and are relatively easy to find and purchase.

Chinchillas are not demanding. However, they do have special needs—including a comfortable and loving home, a spacious cage with hideaways and toys, an exercise wheel, fresh food and water, and a caring owner with plenty of time to visit!

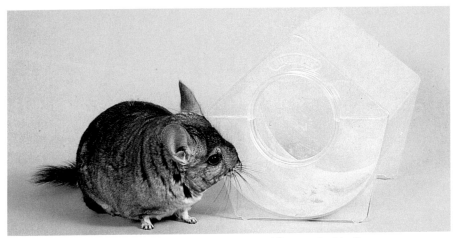

Chinchillas are inquisitive. This one is about to try out its new dust bath.

Companions for Life

Just because chinchillas are small animals does not mean you do not have a lot to consider before you can add one to your family. Responsible pet ownership always involves a certain amount of planning, commitment, time, and expense. In all fairness to yourself and your future pet, you should do your homework *before* you buy your chinchilla so you can learn as much as possible about its special needs and behaviors. To know chinchillas is to love them. Learning all about them will not only help you decide whether a chinchilla is compatible with your lifestyle but also how many you can comfortably house and afford.

Remember that chinchillas can live as long as 20 years—longer than it takes to raise a child and longer than some marriages last! Twenty years is a long time to commit to any animal. So consider your long-range plans.

Are you really ready and willing to accept the responsibility of feeding, cleaning, and caring for a chinchilla for two decades or more? During that time you will probably do one or more of the following: change jobs, go on vacation, start college, move, deal with family obligations, or add a new baby or a new pet to the family. How will a chinchilla fit in with all of this?

If you think a chinchilla will work with your long-range plans, what about short-range plans? Do you have anything planned for the immediate future that might interfere in caring for a pet? If you rent, does your landlord allow pets? Some landlords may not allow cats and dogs but will give permission for smaller caged pets if the tenant pays a modest deposit, so discuss these options with your landlord *before* you buy a chinchilla.

Take everything into consideration, both long and short term, before bringing home a chinchilla. Do not end up in a situation where you can no longer keep your little companion and must give it up for adoption.

Before you bring your chinchilla home, make sure you have everything prepared in advance for its arrival. A little bit of good planning will go a long way to ensure that things go smoothly for you and your new friend during the transition period.

No Two Alike!

Chinchillas are delightful animals, but they vary widely in personalities. Most are active, fun to watch, and will entertain you for hours with their antics. Others are more sedate or less interesting. Many chinchillas enjoy being petted, but many do not want to be handled, no matter how young they were when purchased and no matter how much you try to socialize them. Some animals are at ease being held; others don't like it and struggle to get free. Some chinchillas are very affectionate, and others are indifferent. Chinchillas vary in personality as much as people. So before you bring a chinchilla home, be sure it has the right personality that you want in a pet!

Chinchillas are easy to maintain in captivity if you follow the guidelines in this book for health, nutrition, and housing. They are also very active and need a lot of space to run and play. Here are some things to consider and help you decide if one or

Friend for life! Chinchillas can live up to twenty years. Are you prepared to take on the care and responsibility of a pet for this many years?

more of these acrobatic critters would make a compatible companion for you.

Is a Chinchilla a Good Match for You?

Think about yourself and your family first. How you live and what you do are important factors in assessing how well a chinchilla will fit into your lifestyle. Adding a new pet to the family should always be a happy, positive, stress-free experience.

It is well known that pet ownership has many benefits. For example, people who own animals have been known to derive certain physiological and psychological benefits from the close human-animal bond they form.

Pet owners feel wanted, needed, and loved, and indeed they are. After all, their animals depend on them for food and care, and give affection and companionship in return. Caressing or holding an animal has even been shown to reduce blood pressure in some cases. Medical research suggests that people who own pets may even live longer!

However, owning a pet is not always easy. It is a long-term time commitment and financial responsibility. Do not forget that along with the joys of pet ownership is the sadness that accompanies the eventual, and inevitable, illness, loss, or death of your pet. You can easily become very attached to a chinchilla. Naturally, the longer you have your pet, the more you will love it. Because chinchillas are so responsive and can live so long, when they are gone they are dearly missed. When people buy a new pet, they seldom think about whether the animal may become ill during its life, how much veterinary care might cost, or about the sad day when they will have to part with their precious family pet. These are all important and necessary parts of pet ownership. Anyone thinking about adding a chinchilla to his or her life must be prepared for the inevitable as well as for the fun aspects of owning it.

So, all things considered, are you a good candidate for a chinchilla? Are you ready, willing, and prepared to take on the responsibilities of owning and caring for this enchanting pet for a long, long time?

Chinchilla Expenses

Chinchillas are expensive compared with more common, smaller rodent pets (guinea pigs, rats, mice, hamsters, and gerbils). A pet chinchilla can cost from $50 to more than $100. That is a reasonable price for such a great pet. If your pet lives to be 20 years old, the purchase price of $100 would average out to be only $5 a year! Few such small investments can return so much fun and enjoyment in return!

Some of the more fancy-colored animals bring a higher price. They often cost several hundred dollars. This is especially so if you are purchasing a very attractively colored animal, with outstanding body conformation, for breeding purposes or for exhibiting at the shows.

The purchase price of your chinchilla is not your biggest investment. No matter what your pet's price is, it will be minimal compared with the costs of housing, space, food, and veterinary care over the years. Fortunately, quality chinchilla food is relatively inexpensive and so is the wide variety of toys you can buy or make for your pet.

Your biggest monetary expense will be caging. Buy the most spacious and best-built cage and the best-quality bedding material you can afford. Housing and bedding are two areas in which you should never scrimp when it comes to your pet's health and contentment.

With good care, chinchillas are relatively hardy pets, but it's always a good idea to have some money

Is a chinchilla the right pet for you? Do your homework first and be absolutely sure before you bring a chinchilla into your life.

saved up in case your pet ever needs emergency veterinary care. By saving a small amount each month, veterinary care will be more affordable for you and the funds will be there when you need them.

The major investment you cannot easily measure is time. Set aside time to play with your chinchilla every day. This contact is important to keep your companion happy and well socialized. Chinchillas love to visit with their owners. You must also take time to give fresh food and water every day and to clean the cage at least once a week. The amount of time and money you spend taking care of your little friend is small compared with the fun and affection it will give you in return.

Doing these is a wise investment to ensure that your bright-eyed companion is healthy and happy.

Other Household Pets

One of the biggest threats to a chinchilla's safety is the presence of another animal. Chinchillas have very keen senses of hearing and smell. They know when other animals are in the house and can become stressed or frightened if your other pets come near the cage. Make sure the door to the cage is securely fastened. Be sure to place the cage well out of reach of the family dog, cat, ferret, bird, or any other pet. You probably never thought of your house pets as being harmful, but cats and ferrets are natural hunters and dogs can

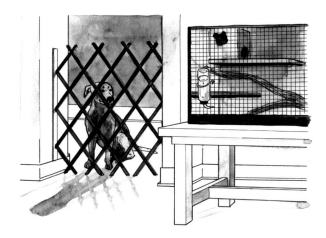

Make sure your chinchilla is out of reach of other household pets. Chinchillas can be seriously injured by other animals.

play roughly. Even large birds can peck a small animal to death. Many household pets will not bother an adult chinchilla due to its relatively large size. However, kits are quite vulnerable to attacks by other animals, and a large pet reptile would find a baby chinchilla very tasty indeed. Although chinchillas can inflict serious bite wounds when frightened, they are no match for larger, predator-type animals.

Many people who keep chinchillas also keep other species of rodent pets. *Do not house your chinchilla with other rodents.* Chinchillas live in harmony in the wild with other rodent species native to their country (such as degus and chinchilla rats), but they do not naturally live with rodents kept commonly as pets. Rodent pets are likely to bite. You may find your chinchilla's ears partially nibbled off or a deep puncture wound on its back. Also, chinchillas are susceptible to many rodent diseases that can be carried by and shared with other

rodent pets. Your other rodents may not appear ill, but they can spread infections to your chinchilla that can make it very sick.

Do not house your chinchilla with rabbits. They may spread serious diseases to chinchillas, such as *Bordetella* (see "Chinchilla Health Care").

Another problem with housing other pet species and chinchillas together is that your chin may eat the other animals' food, and you *do not* want that to happen! Chinchillas have sensitive gastrointestinal tracts, and an unbalanced diet can cause serious health problems (see "Feeding Your Chinchilla"). For the safety of all the pets in your household, and in the best interests of your chinchilla's health, house your chins separately from other species and keep them out of reach of other animals.

Can You Chinchilla Proof Your Home?

Some of the more fun aspects of chinchillas—their small size, inquisitiveness, speed, and agility—create some of the biggest problems for their safety. And don't let all that fur fool you! Chinchillas are smaller than their dense, plush coat makes them look. They can fit through all kinds of small spaces. After all, they are burrowing animals. If your chin can squeeze its broad head through an opening, the rest of its body will follow easily. Because chinchillas are rodents and rodents love to chew, you cannot keep them in wooden, plastic, or cardboard containers. They will eventually gnaw their way out and escape. Escaping is one of the things chinchillas do best! They are superb escape artists!

Accidents happen. Someone may fail to latch your pet's cage door securely, or it may find a way to escape. Whatever the circumstances, once your pet is loose in your home, it faces countless life-threatening situations, such as exposure to household chemicals, pesticides, rodent traps, electrical shock, bite wounds from other pets, crushing injuries, and limb fractures from ricocheting off objects when they panic.

To prevent accident and injury, make sure to take the time to make your house safe for your pet *before* it comes home (see "Your Chinchilla Comes Home"). Always supervise it every second that it is out of its cage!

A Noisy Pet

Do not let that soft, mild-mannered appearance fool you! Chinchillas can be very noisy. They have

Caging will be one of your biggest monetary investments. Buy a cage big enough to give your chinchilla(s) lots of room to run and play.

a wide range of vocalizations (see "Understanding Your Chinchilla") and can be quite "talkative" at times. When they are not calling or "conversing," they are often busy creating other noises in their cage. Be sure to put your chinchilla's cage in an area where it will not disturb you when you need some peace and quiet!

Aaachooo! Tips for the Allergy Prone

Allergies to animals are quite common. Some people simply cannot have pets, no matter how much they love them. For example, people with allergies or with compromised or suppressed immune systems can jeopardize their health by adding more allergens (substances that cause allergies), such as pet dander, urine, cage bedding, dust, and hay, to their environment.

Rodents are among the more allergenic (causing allergies) of pets. The allergen responsible for causing most allergies to rodents is urine, not hair as most people think. Owners are exposed to rodent urine every time they change the cage. Eventually, after repeated exposures, allergy-prone individuals develop a specific sensitivity to rodent urine, as well as to rodent dander. In fact, allergies to animals are occupational hazards of veterinarians and laboratory workers.

Allergies usually develop over a long period of time and exposure. In other words, you may not be allergic to chinchillas right now because you may not have had a lot of exposure to them, but what about later? You certainly do not want to develop an allergy later on and have to part with your pet.

Check with your physician to determine if you are allergy prone. If your doctor gives you the go-ahead on owning a pet, first visit some chinchilla breeders, pet shops, or friends who own chinchillas. Try holding and petting a chinchilla and linger awhile. Go back and visit several times. If you develop any signs of an allergy—itchy and watery eyes, shortness of breath, rash, wheezing, coughing, or sneezing—then do not bring a chinchilla into your home. You risk harming your health and will eventually have to give up your pet for adoption.

On the other hand, if you do not have signs of allergies, you can take some precautions to reduce the chances of developing an allergy in the future.

• Do not keep your pet's cage in the bedroom, where you would have close exposure to it for several hours each evening. There is no sense in unnecessarily exposing yourself to allergens while you are sleeping!

• Place your pet's cage in a well-ventilated, but not drafty, area of the house.

• Invest in an air filter. HEPA-filtered air cleaners are excellent at keeping air fresh and free of dander and dust.

• Place absorbent paper underneath the bedding material. Absorbent

If you are allergy prone, giving your pet an enclosed dust bath container will reduce your exposure to the dust. Even a fish bowl can work for dust baths.

paper is one of the best ways possible to lower exposure to allergy-causing substances, especially urine.

• Wear a mask and gloves when changing your pet's bedding. This might seem a bit extreme or dramatic, but it greatly reduces your chances of exposure to allergens. Gloves and a mask help prevent exposure through inhalation or contact. (If you use gloves, vinyl gloves are recommended instead of latex gloves because many people are allergic to latex.)

• Take the cage outside to clean it if possible. This prevents small particles from scattering throughout the house. In addition to urine, house mites (that can get into bedding) and wood shavings often cause allergies.

• Make sure your chinchilla takes dust baths in closed containers or closed dust bins specially designed for chinchillas, rather than in open bins, bowls, or pans.

Children and Chinchillas

Chinchillas make wonderful pets for adults, but they are not ideal pets for young children because they are difficult to hold or restrain and can

Improper handling can cause loss of fur and ruin a beautiful coat.

easily slip free, fall, and be injured. Sudden movements or loud sounds may startle a chinchilla, and it may squirm about and escape. Unfortunately, most chinchillas that are dropped are seriously injured. Even a fall from a short distance often results in a broken leg, usually involving the tibia (a long bone in the hind leg). Also, chinchillas will not hesitate to bite if they feel threatened or are frightened. Chinchillas have large, powerful teeth that can inflict deep, painful, puncture wounds or remove the tips of small fingers—and they are fast! *Chinchillas should be handled with caution and respect as well as with care!*

Chinchillas are definitely more suited to adults, but that does not mean young children cannot enjoy them. Children simply must learn that it is safer for the animal and for them if they observe the chinchilla in the cage. Children naturally love cute, soft, furry animals, and chinchillas are very entertaining. Watching chinchilla activities is a lot of fun. Children can learn a lot about animal behavior, animal care, kindness, and responsibility. All that is required is adult supervision for the safety of the child and the pet, and then everyone can enjoy themselves!

To prevent injury to your pet, anyone in the family who will be handling it must learn the correct way to pick it up, hold it comfortably, and restrain it when necessary. The safety of children, family members, and your pet is *your* responsibility. When you cannot be there to supervise activities, make sure children understand the cage is off limits in your absence and make sure the cage door is fastened

Children should always be supervised when playing with a pet. Take time to teach children the correct way to hold a chinchilla. This will help prevent injury.

securely. This is a safety measure well worth the temporary inconvenience.

Completely Charmed

Some children are uncomfortable around animals, especially large ones. Children who have had a bad experience with animals in the past, such as having suffered a dog bite or a cat scratch, can greatly benefit from getting to know a chinchilla. This soft, beautiful, bright-eyed animal can completely charm a child and change fear into affection and interest. You cannot ask for a better confidence builder!

With adult guidance, the things children can learn from a chinchilla are unlimited. Their very presence offers an excellent opportunity for adults to teach children about pets, the importance of humane care and treatment, and respect for life. Young children can learn about the importance of fresh water, good food, and a clean home. This can help children develop a sense of responsibility.

Depending on their ages, children can learn about animal behavior, sleep patterns, exercise, nutrition, biology, reproduction, and even color genetics. In fact, older children can turn the knowledge they gain from chinchilla ownership into a school science project or a 4-H project. After all, some of these young chinchilla aficionados may one day become reputable, respected chinchilla breeders and exhibitors in the not-too-distant future, and we will need them to supply us with more of these adorable animals!

Chapter Three

Choosing the Perfect Chinchilla

After doing your homework and thinking things through, you have decided a chinchilla is the right pet for you. Great! Now it's time to find the perfect chinchilla—and they are all so different that you will want to look at several before you choose the best match for you. During your search, keep in mind that *the health, personality, and age of your pet are more important than its color.*

Where to Find a Chinchilla

Chinchillas are fairly easy to find. The best way to find a healthy, attractive, well-socialized, easy-to-handle chinchilla is to purchase one from a reputable chinchilla breeder. Experienced breeders know their animals' genetics, ages, socialization conditions, and breeding and health records. Breeders usually have a nice selection of beautifully colored chinchillas available. If you want a rare or unusual-colored chinchilla, you will probably have to make a special request far in advance of when you expect to make your pur-

chase. Special orders cannot always be filled immediately. However, if you are patient, the right animal will come your way and will be well worth the wait.

If you are thinking about raising chinchillas, as a hobbyist or professionally, then you definitely must consult and buy from an experienced, successful chinchilla breeder. You should also seriously reconsider your reasons for wanting to be a chinchilla breeder (see "Raising Chinchillas") and be certain it is the right activity for you.

For a list of breeders in your area, contact the Empress Chinchilla Breeders Cooperative or the Mutation Chinchilla Breeders Association (see "Useful Addresses and Literature"). They can give you the name, address, and telephone number of chinchilla associations and breeders in your state. You can also find chinchilla breeders in many pet magazines (available in bookstores and pet shops) that advertise pets for sale.

Pet shops often have chinchillas for sale. They are usually animals that breeders did not keep for breeding stock because they did not meet the high standards of conformation and pelt quality required for exhibition and competition. Any conformational "flaws" a pet shop chinchilla might have would not be obvious to the untrained eye and would not matter to someone who is just looking for a pet to love. A chinchilla does not have to be a champion to be an attractive, adorable pet. On the other hand, if the chinchilla in the pet shop is very old, cannot be handled, or has an unpleasant disposition, that is a different matter. If you are thinking about buying a chinchilla from a pet shop, take your time and do not make a snap decision. Be sure to ask how long the animal has been in the store, if it is tame and can be handled, if it is healthy, how old it is, if it has been tested for parasites, and if it has a medical record. Spend lots of time with it and hold it. Watch how it responds to you and its surrounding environment. If the animal is not tame or is difficult to hold, if it is aggressive and tries to bite, or if it does not appear healthy, do not buy it.

Another way to find a chinchilla is to check the local newspaper classified section for advertisements. Sometimes people have nice animals

that they must give up for adoption for various reasons.

Your veterinarian may also know some chinchilla breeders you can contact. Or, if you know someone who owns a chinchilla, ask where the animal was purchased. Word of mouth is often the best referral.

Finally, you can always find chinchilla breeders on the Internet and by visiting chinchilla web sites. Just remember that there are always risks associated with buying an animal sight unseen on the Internet. If you do not know the seller, ask for references, photos of the animal, and health guarantees.

No matter where you live, there is bound to be a chinchilla that is perfect for you just waiting for you to find it!

Help! Chinchilla Rescue

Sometimes you can find a nice chinchilla at the local animal shelter or with the help of a rescue group. These poor animals are in the shelter through no fault of their own. They may be well mannered and good natured. However, because their owners could no longer keep them and did not take the time to find them a new home personally, they have been abandoned or relinquished to the shelter. Often chinchillas are given up for adoption because their owners moved, or the landlord did not allow pets, or the family or job situation changed. Less frequently, allergy is the culprit. Sometimes chinchillas are left at animal shelters because their owners

Chinchilla Contacts
- Chinchilla breeders associations
- Local chinchilla breeders
- Pet stores
- Veterinarians
- Internet web sites
- Advertisements in pet magazines
- Animal shelters
- Newspaper advertisements

Chinchillas adopted from animal shelters often need more time to adapt to a new home.

Chinchillas adopted from animal shelters often need more time to adapt to a new home.

did not learn about what chinchilla care and ownership involved before they acquired the animals and now find that it is more responsibility than they can manage.

All relinquished animals have one thing in common. They desperately need a loving, caring home. Before you adopt a chinchilla at the animal shelter, be sure to talk to the adoption counselor and learn as much as you can about it to be sure it will work out for you. Chinchillas can be set in their ways, and there may be some definite challenges to adopting an adult. For example, a chinchilla that has not been handled daily will need some reassurance and an extra amount of socialization. It may never enjoy handling or become completely tame, no matter how much time you spend with it or how hard you try.

If you think a relinquished adult chinchilla could make a good companion for you, visit your local animal shelter. Take along a list of all of your questions to ask the adoption counselors.

The counselors can give you detailed information on each animal in their care. Be prepared to answer some questions about yourself as well. Just as you are looking for the perfect chinchilla, the adoption counselors are looking for the perfect person for the animal in their care. They want to be sure that it will never have

to change homes and families ever again!

Chinchilla Choices

Few things are as cute as a young chinchilla. Unless you are planning on raising chinchillas and want to purchase adults from the onset, a youngster is the best way to go. It will quickly adapt to your home life, and you will have most of its lifetime to enjoy it. Be honest—they are much cuter, too!

The best way to find a good-natured, healthy, attractive, young chinchilla is to visit a reputable chinchilla breeder. Chinchillas are very well developed at birth, and their eyes are wide open. They are weaned by four months of age and should not leave their mother before this time. Try to find a weanling that is not much older than four months of age. Do not be an impulse buyer! The first (and second and third!) chinchilla you see will certainly tug at your heartstrings and you will want to buy it. Resist the temptation until you can visit as many breeders as possible. Look at as many animals as you can *before* you make a selection. This way you can compare the overall health and quality of the animals, the cleanliness of their environments, their sociability, the different colors, and the different price ranges.

Never buy a chinchilla because you feel sorry for it. Animals that draw our sympathy—animals that are undersized, thin, scraggly, or withdrawn—are the ones that are unwell and may cause you heartache later on. It is human nature to want to reach out to these unfortunate crea-tures and help them. You imagine how much better they would be under your personal care. Focus on your goal, though, to find a bright-eyed, healthy, active companion with a bubbly personality. Unless you are prepared for the time commitment, veterinary expenses, and disappointments that may accompany a sick or hapless animal, look for the healthiest, friendliest, and most inquisitive chinchilla you can find.

Choosing a Healthy Chinchilla

A healthy chinchilla is bright-eyed, alert, and interested in its surroundings—and it is interested in *you*. When you approach, it should come up to greet you and investigate. If the little character is tame (and a little bit spoiled!), it will probably be looking for a treat along with a caress!

Healthy chinchillas have good appetites and are inquisitive and active. They nap for short periods of time, several times, throughout the day and night. If your pet seems to be sleeping most of the time, it is a sign that something is wrong.

A sick chinchilla is quiet, listless, and dull. It may sit hunched up in a corner, away from all the activity, avoiding you and its fellow cage mates. Hair loss, weight loss, and loss of interest in its surroundings are signs of illness. Panting, sneezing, wheezing, coughing, discharge (from the eyes, ears, nose, mouth, or anus), diarrhea, constipation, lack of

Use Good Judgment: Do Not Buy for Others and Do Not Buy During the Holidays!

Animals are often purchased as gifts, especially during the holidays. This act of generosity can be disastrous for a chinchilla.

• First, although it is tempting, it is a bad idea to buy an animal as a gift. People who want pets also want the fun of *personally* selecting their own pets.

• Second, not everyone wants to assume the responsibility of pet ownership. Chinchilla ownership is a tremendous responsibility because of the animal's 20-year life span and the time, space, and commitment a chinchilla requires.

• Third, the holiday season is not a good time to add a pet to the family. This is a time when most people already have plenty to do with visitors, deadlines, and commitments. A new pet can be overlooked in the busy shuffle with all the distractions and excitement. Families do not have time to learn about, observe, socialize, and care for a new pet during the holidays. Visitors and guests unfamiliar with proper handling techniques may stress and frighten the new arrival or drop it. Someone may forget to close the cage door. Holidays are a time when many pets escape from home or are lost.

• Finally, pets bought during the holidays may be shipped great distances in bad weather, prone to illness, and suffering from stress. All of these can lead to sickness or death. There are, of course, animal protection laws. However, you should be aware of, and avoid, potential problems.

bowel movements, and convulsing, or other nervous system problems, are all signs of a sick animal.

Never buy a chinchilla that was housed in a cage where another animal showed signs of illness. The sick animal may have a contagious disease. If you buy a chinchilla that was exposed to a sick chinchilla, your pet could be incubating the disease and fall ill a few days after you bring it home.

Once you have chosen a healthy chinchilla to take home, ask if you can pick it up and hold it before you buy it. You will quickly learn how much handling the animal has had and how mild mannered it is by its behavior. If it squirms and wiggles to free itself, hold it firmly but gently against your chest. Do not let it fall. Speak to it softly and reassuringly. Give it a little bit of time to calm down and get used to you. If it does not relax after a few minutes or if it acts aggressively or tries to bite, continue your search for a more socialized, tame individual!

If the animal you have selected is calm and allows you to hold it gently, examine it closely to be sure it is in good health. The eyes should be bright and clear. Ears should be clean, and skin and hair should look healthy. Bald patches and poor coat condition may mean the animal is sick or has a skin problem or parasites. Examine the belly and the bot-

Choose a chinchilla with clear, bright eyes, a beautiful coat, and an outgoing personality. The more friendly and inquisitive, the better.

colored teeth are not normal and are signs of health problems. Check that the teeth are properly aligned in the mouth. Dental misalignment causes many health problems and is usually an inherited problem. *Animals with crooked, misdirected teeth should never be used for breeding.*

If you already have chinchillas at home, keep the new animal isolated from the others for at least one week to make sure it is not incubating a contagious disease. This will prevent accidental spread of disease to your other pets in case your new chinchilla develops an unexpected, contagious health problem.

Chinchilla Health Check

• Are the eyes bright and clear? They should be dark in color (black or brown) or dark ruby red.
• Is the coat plush, dense, and shiny?
• Is the skin healthy and free of parasites?
• Is the animal behaving normally?
• Does it move, hop, run, leap, stand, and sit normally?
• Does the animal curl its tail and carry it high?
• Is it alert, active, inquisitive, and friendly?
• Is it the right weight (not too thin and not too heavy)?
• Check under the tail for signs of diarrhea or staining.
• Check the mouth, eyes, ears, nose, anus, and genital area for signs of discharge.
• Are the teeth (incisors) properly aligned and are they yellow?

tom of the feet to be sure there are no sores on them. Make sure the animal sits and walks in a normal manner, and take the time to observe that it is eating and drinking.

One of the most important indicators of a healthy chinchilla is the presence of normal fecal pellets. Absence of fecal pellets, or the presence of small, dry pellets or diarrhea, are signs of health problems.

Examine the front teeth. This is easier said than done, especially if your chinchilla does not allow you to restrain it or examine its mouth. The teeth should be light to dark yellow. White, orange, brown, black, or dis-

- Check for sores on the feet.
- Is the animal pregnant?

The chinchilla you finally select will depend on availability, physical qualities, and your personal preferences. Of all the animals you have visited, which ones appeal the most to you? Which are the most friendly, healthy, curious, and playful? Which ones have the most personality? Which ones enjoy being held, petted, or snuggled close to you? Which ones are the most attractive and irresistible? The hardest thing about choosing a chinchilla to join your family is leaving the other ones behind! This brings us to the next question: is one enough?

Joining a chinchilla club and attending chinchilla shows are a lot of fun.

How Many Chinchillas to Keep?

How many chinchillas you keep is purely up to you. It depends a lot on your reasons for owning a chinchilla and your available time, space, and money. Chinchilla ownership should be fun. If you have so many animals that you seem to spend more time cleaning up after them than enjoying them, then you have too many! Start conservatively with just one animal. Later on, if you find you have more time, space, knowledge, funds, enthusiasm, and love to share, you may eventually accumulate an entire herd!

Of course, if you know you want to raise chinchillas as a hobby, you will need to buy at least one male and one female or, more likely, one male and two or three females to start. In this case, a reputable breeder will be a valuable source of information and animals for you. An experienced breeder can answer many questions about chinchilla husbandry, colors, behavior, and resources. A breeder will have the latest information about chinchilla clubs, shows, and activities in your area. Clubs are a great way to meet other people who share your interests, and they are a lot of fun.

Keep your animal numbers reasonable so you have time to spend with your pets and to enjoy them. The number you keep all depends on your lifestyle, how much housing space you can provide, whether you want to raise and exhibit chinchillas, and the amount of time you can dedicate to cultivating your friendship with these charming beings.

A single chinchilla can be great company and provide hours of entertainment. Chinchillas can become quite attached to their owners and not only enjoy human interaction but demand it. If you spend lots of time caressing, holding, and playing with your pet, it will be perfectly happy to be an only child and not miss being with other chinchillas. However, in all fairness to your pet, remember that chinchillas are colonial animals that normally live in family units. Without social interaction with you, your chin can become lonely and bored. So if your schedule requires long or frequent absences, you should keep a minimum of two compatible animals to keep each other company.

Chinchillas do well in small family pairs. If you house animals together, make sure they are compatible. It is best if they have known each other from a very early age. For example, male littermates can usually be housed together peacefully as long as no females are in the area, and mother-daughter or female sibling pairs also work well. By housing compatible animals of the same sex together, you can prevent fights and injuries, as well as unwanted pregnancies.

Male or Female?

The decision whether to own a male or a female depends on your personal preference. If you are simply looking for a wonderful pet and an interesting companion, you will be happy with either one. If you are planning to raise chinchillas, you obviously need at least one pair to begin your project.

The main physical difference you will note is that the female is larger (approximately 1.77 pounds [800 g]) than the male (approximately 1.3 pounds [600 g]). Otherwise, the anatomical differences are subtle, except that mature males have large testicles that are retained in the inguinal canal. Chinchillas do not have a true scrotum. The inguinal canal is open, and the epididymis (a cordlike structure where spermatozoa are stored and mature that is attached to the testicle) drops into a postanal sac.

Your pet's individual personality has as much, or more, to do with the kind and gentle way it is raised than with its gender. Most chin-chillas that are handled often and tamed as babies are sweet, social, and affectionate.

A Long-term Commitment

Chinchillas live a long time, some-times more than 20 years. Longevity varies with each individual animal and is influenced by the care and nutrition it receives.

Two decades is a long time to be responsible for an animal's care, and that responsibility is all yours! Never rely on children to take care of a pet. Children change interests, grow up, leave home, and go to college. Do not expect others to accept the responsibility of caring for your pet. For many adults and children, the novelty of a new pet wears off shortly after the animal's arrival. *If you bring a chinchilla into your home, be pre-pared to be its sole caretaker for its very long life!*

Coat Color

Chinchillas come in a variety of beautiful coat colors, including blue-gray, silver-gray, gray, white, black, charcoal, beige, and a wide range of color variations in between! They can be more than one color, such as white and beige, black and white, or charcoal and white. The colors can be separated, as in an animal with a black body and a white underbelly, or the colors can be blotched,

Chinchillas come in a wide variety of colors. Mosaic chinchillas, like this one, are very popular.

splotched, or mottled throughout the coat in a mosaic pattern.

Chinchilla Charisma

Every chinchilla has its individual personality and special charm. As you visit breeders, chinchilla shows, pet shops, and shelters in your search for the ideal companion, you will be delighted at the variety of cheerful, playful chinchilla personali-ties you encounter. Whether you are looking for a companion or a show prospect, you will be drawn to one special animal because of its unique character and qualities. The chinchilla that radiates a winning personality and is eager to bond with you is the chinchilla you will choose to warm your heart and brighten your home.

Chapter Four

Housing

You do not have to duplicate the rugged, high desert, mountainous terrains of the West Andes of Chile to make your chinchilla feel at home. However, knowledge about chinchilla lifestyle in the wild gives us some useful insights and helpful tips on how to keep our domestic chins happy and healthy in captivity.

Natural Habitat

The few chinchillas remaining in the wild live in barren, arid mountain chains at elevations ranging from sea level to 5,400 feet (1,650 m). Until they were hunted to near extinction in the late 1800s, chinchillas historically inhabited a larger geographic area, including the western slopes of the Andes and parts of Bolivia, Peru, and Argentina. Chinchillas lived between sea level and altitudes as high as 15,000 feet (4,572 m), where temperatures fluctuated from room temperature to below freezing. Depending on altitude and wind chill factor, temperatures often averaged slightly above freezing. This, how-

Chinchillas love their homes and hideaways and feel safe and secure in them.

ever, does not mean that chinchillas can tolerate freezing temperatures—they cannot. In the wild, chinchillas remain in their thermal comfortable burrows when the weather is uncomfortably cold.

In their native habitat, chinchillas are territorial, social, active, cursorial (meaning their legs are well adapted for running), and acrobatic! They take shelter in rock crevices and burrows, where they hide from predators such as foxes and owls. They use large rocks as lookout posts, resting platforms, and toilet areas. Chinchilla burrows are well hidden among the rocks and usually consist of an entry that leads to a long tunnel that turns and opens into a large sleeping area or dormitory. Food and grass bedding can sometimes be found stored in burrows.

Chinchillas coexist peacefully with other small animals of their region, including small South American marsupials (*Thylamys elegans*) and their distant hystricomorph rodent cousins, the degu (*Octodon degus*) and the chinchilla rat (*Abrocoma bennetti*).

Chinchillas are philopatric, meaning they love their home and its surrounding area. Studies have shown that chinchillas will stay in a small area for as long as six years. This is important to know, because it means that if you give your pet what it needs for a safe and comfortable home, it will be very happy to stay and live there!

Housing Considerations

There are a lot of things to think about as you plan the perfect "home sweet home" for your pet. Your choice of housing will depend on the number of animals you keep, your available time and space, and cage style preferences, size, and location.

Chinchillas are social and colonial. If given the opportunity, they would naturally live in family units. Chinchillas can also be aggressive, territorial, and domineering toward outsiders. If they are not compatible, chinchillas will fight and can seriously injure or kill one another. Females can be especially aggressive toward males.

Fortunately, chinchillas are quite content to live alone. As long as you give your pet lots of attention, space, hideaways, toys, and fresh food and water, it will be happy.

Material

Chinchillas, like all rodents, have sharp, strong teeth and love to chew. This means that they can chew their way out of almost anything, especially wood and plastic cages! Your chin's home must be very sturdy and made of material strong enough to resist chewing, digging, tunneling, and unauthorized exit or entry. Only wire mesh will do for chinchilla chambers.

Chinchillas are very entertaining. When you are not cuddling your pet, you will enjoy watching it. Wire cage material allows good visibility so you can easily observe your pet. It is also strong, nonporous, easy to clean, and allows for good air circulation.

Wire mesh for housing adults should be 1 inch × 1 inch (25 mm × 25 mm), or ½ inch × 1 inch (12.5 mm × 25 mm). Baby chinchillas need a small grid mesh to prevent their feet and limbs from falling through the gaps and being trapped and broken (a common injury in baby chinchillas housed on wire mesh that is too large). Wire mesh for housing baby chinchillas should be ¾ inch × ¾ inch (20 mm × 20 mm) or ½ inch × 1 inch (12.5 mm × 25 mm).

Some cleaning solutions can strip the wire of galvanized mesh and result in rusting over time. Rusty cage mesh can weaken and break,

Chinchillas love to play in tunnels. You can make toy tunnels from PVC plumbing pipes.

leading to injury or escape. Check the cage well when you clean it, do not use caustic cleaners, and always rinse the cage well.

Size

Chinchillas need a lot of space. They can jump, leap, and bound with amazing agility and speed. The cage must be large enough to give your pet plenty of room to run, play, and exercise; to provide for a toilet area; and to contain all of your pet's toys, dishes, feeders, hideaways, tunnels, shelves, running wheel, platform rocks, tree branches, chew sticks, and other necessary objects. The cage should also be large enough to allow good ventilation. When deciding how big your pet's cage should be, remember that wire mesh cages are heavy and the bigger the cage,

the heavier it is. Moving or transporting a large wire mesh cage can be difficult.

Cage size depends on the number of animals you house and the amount of space available in your home. If you are breeding and raising chinchillas, you will need more cages and space than if you are keeping just one or two as companions (see "Raising Chinchillas").

At a bare minimum, cage size for one chinchilla should be no less than 16 inches (35 cm) wide, 18 inches (40 cm) long, and 16 inches (35 cm) high. Colony cages should be at least 3 feet (1 m) long, 1.5 feet (50 cm) high, and 1.5 feet (50 cm) wide. If you can give your pet a bigger cage, that is even better!

Cage doors and lids should latch securely to prevent escape (a com-

Plastic toys are colorful and easy to clean, but your chinchilla will chew on them. Supervise your pet when it plays with them and remove them after playtime.

mon occurrence!). They should be large enough that you can easily reach into the cage comfortably to catch your chinchilla, clean the cage, or add and remove large objects, such as shelves, an exercise wheel, or tube tunnels.

You will find that when your chinchilla has enough room, it will run around and leap when it plays. The price of a larger cage will be offset by the hours of entertainment your pet will give you!

Style

Cage style is limited only by your imagination. Your pet will be perfectly happy in a simple, single,

Travel Cage

For relocating or transporting your pet (for example, when cleaning the home cage or taking your pet to the veterinarian, to shows, or in case of emergency), purchase a small travel cage or cat flight kennel.

one-story cage. You can also choose from a large variety of cage styles that will make life more interesting.

Single story: You can choose from a large variety of single-story cages. You can also buy a double cage that consists of two single-story cages that share a middle divider and a door that can be opened or closed between the two cages. This type of arrangement is ideal for housing two animals together, yet keeping them apart until you know they are compatible. If you keep only one animal in the double cage, cleaning the cage is easier and the chances of your chinchilla escaping are reduced because you can close your pet securely in one of the sides of the cage while you clean the open side.

Double story: A two-story cage is taller and has ramps and shelves that lead to the upper level. Chinchillas do not necessarily need ramps because they are capable of jumping on and off shelves and platforms with ease. They like to sit up on the highest platform where they can be on the lookout.

Multitiered cage: A cage can have additional third or fourth levels. These kinds of cages must be very large to accommodate adult animals. Although they are more interesting and give your pet a lot more space to exercise and play, they also make catching your pet when you need to examine it or want to take it out of the cage more difficult.

Stacked cages: Commercial chinchilla farmers house their animals in stacked cages, often in rows of three. Chinchillas on the bottom row receive less light and ventilation than those on the upper rows, and they also feel more threatened and are more stressed. If you plan to keep your pets in stacked cages, they may do better if you rotate them weekly so that the same animal does not always have to live on the bottom row.

Indoors Only!

Pet chinchillas should be kept indoors where the temperature and humidity can be controlled, where they are free from flies and wild rodents that can transmit diseases, and where they can watch all the family activities. If you must keep your pet outdoors, find a safe place for the cage in a well-protected, sheltered area out of the wind and sun. Shade should be available at all times throughout the day. Make sure that the cage is out of reach of other pets (dogs, cats, ferrets, birds) or

The size and style of cage and the number of cages you purchase all depend on the number of chinchillas you decide to house.

Spacious Accommodations

If your pet's cage is spacious enough to accommodate it comfortably with room enough to play and enough space for hideaways, toys, exercise wheel, tunnels, dishes, bottles, resting board, shelves, dust bins, and other chinchilla essentials, then you have done a great job!

wild animals and birds (raccoons, skunks, opossums, coyotes, hawks, owls). Your gentle chin is no match for these predators.

Wire Floors and Foot Sores

Wire mesh cage floors can be hard on delicate chinchilla legs, feet, and toes. Crinkle wire mesh is even more damaging to feet than regular wire mesh and should not be used for chinchilla cages.

Chinchilla feet are sensitive. Wire mesh is irritating and can cause painful foot sores and ulcerations. Ideally, the cage you purchase should have a solid bottom floor or floor pan

Baby Feet

Do not house baby chinchillas on wire mesh floors. Their tiny feet and slender limbs can slip through the wire bottom floor and get caught, injured, and broken. Cages for baby chinchillas should always have solid bottom floors to prevent accident and injury.

so that your pet does not develop foot sores. If your cage has a wire floor, you can cushion the wire by placing newspaper or bedding on top of the wire, or directly underneath the wire, so that the animal's weight is supported by soft bedding and not supported by wire.

Protect those dainty feet from injury! Give your chinchilla a resting place to sit on, such as a large, flat rock or a flat piece of nonresinous wood. Wood should be free of nails, nontoxic, and not chemically treated. Wooden boards made from aspen, birch, peach, or apple trees are best. *Do not give your pet cedar or redwood boards.* They contain volatile oils and substances that are harmful for chinchillas.

Avoid Overcrowding

Why do chinchillas require more space than most rodent pets?
• They are larger and more active than most rodents.
• They do not tolerate overcrowding and become stressed if they are

The cage should be large enough to accommodate all of your pet's toys: chew treats, dishes, hideaways, exercise wheel, and tunnels.

housed in cramped quarters. They need their space!
- Chinchillas are content in small family units. More animals housed together require more space.
- Chinchillas do not tolerate heat well and are prone to heatstroke. They are good at conserving body heat but poor at dissipating heat. Too many chinchillas crowded together can overheat—and fight! On a warm day in an overcrowded pen, your pets could become so overheated that they could die of heatstroke.

Environmental Considerations

You must provide your chinchilla with certain environmental considerations. Without the proper temperature, humidity, ventilation, and lighting, your chin will not thrive.

Temperature and Humidity

It is very important to place your pet's cage in an area where the humidity is as low as possible: 30 to 50 percent humidity is ideal for chinchillas. Airborne microorganisms that may cause diseases do not survive well at this humidity. If you live in a humid environment, installing a dehumidifier can make your chin (and you, too!) more comfortable.

Chinchillas do well at temperatures between 63 and 77°F (17 and 25°C). They are very sensitive to heat and are prone to heatstroke. They must be housed at temperatures below 90°F (32°C). High humidity

increases their chances of heat-stroke. If you live in a humid area, your pet should be housed at temperatures below 80°F (27°C).

Just as chinchillas cannot tolerate heat, they also cannot tolerate temperatures at or below freezing. Chinchillas are cherished for their beautiful coats. Their coats grow longer and denser when they are housed at temperatures ranging from 43 to 53°F (5 to 12°C) and at less than 50 percent humidity.

Never place your pet's cage near heaters, radiators, or fans, in areas of direct sunlight, or in the way of drafts.

Ventilation and Lighting

Fresh air is important. Chinchillas need a well-ventilated, but not windy or drafty, environment. If your pet's housing setup is sophisticated enough to measure air exchange rates (most are not), eight air changes per hour in the winter and 15 air changes per hour in the summer are ideal for chinchillas. Even if you do not have a way to measure air exchange rates, you can tell if the air is stuffy and if your pet does not have enough ventilation. A fan to help circulate the air is very useful; just be sure it is not blowing directly on the animal.

Although they can tolerate cold weather better than they can tolerate the heat, chinchillas are very sensitive to cold, damp, drafty conditions. They can develop respiratory (lung) problems and quickly develop pneumonia and die. Their housing should be protected from drafts, cold, and dampness.

Chinchillas are nocturnal and crepuscular. *Nocturnal* means they are most active during the evening. *Crepuscular* refers to their periods of activity in the morning and late afternoon. The word *crepuscular* comes from the French word *crépuscule*, meaning "twilight." So that your pet can rest when it wants during the daytime hours, its cage should be placed in an area of your home that is not too bright during the day and is dark at night. The best lighting schedule is 12 hours of light during the day and 12 hours of dark at night, but you do not have to follow such a strict schedule if it is not convenient for you.

Inside the Cage

What is inside your chinchilla's cage is very important. Include items that will make your chin emotionally satisfied.

Bedding Material

Chinchillas are capable of concentrating their urine to conserve water and minerals. As a result, urine can have an odor and also form deposits (scales) on the cage floor. Mineral scales can be dissolved with vinegar. Choosing the best, cleanest, most absorbent bedding material you can afford will help keep odors to a minimum.

Several kinds of bedding material are commercially available. These include wood shavings, recycled shredded or pelleted paper by-products, grass hay, wood chips, sawdust, fuller's earth, pelleted cat litter (nonclumping and nonscented), ground corncobs, newspaper, and chopped straw (use only chopped grass hay or straw because hay or straw that contains small, sharp, sticklike particles can injure your pet's eyes).

Every type of bedding has advantages and disadvantages. The kind of cage bedding material you choose depends on convenience, cleanliness, and cost.

Pelleted and shredded paper make excellent bedding and are highly recommended, but they are more costly. Wood shavings smell pleasant and absorb urine and odors. They are also more affordable than the recommended paper products, but there are many good reasons not to use them:

• Chinchillas may chew on the shavings and eat them. This can lead to serious health problems, such as gastrointestinal obstruction.

• Some wood shavings have sharp particles and are abrasive and cause foot sores (pododermatitis).

• Particles found in wood shavings may get into your pet's eyes and injure them.

• Fine dust from wood shavings irritates the lungs and leads to allergies—not just for your pets but for you as well!

• Many types of wood shavings, such as pine and cedar, contain substances and volatile oils that can

cause health conditions, including liver problems, allergies, and skin problems.

Corncob bedding is not recommended because it tends to be very drying to the skin and can be dehydrating, especially for kits and very young chins. Do not use clay cat litter for bedding material, especially clumping or scented products. They are dangerous to your pet's health, especially if they are eaten (ingested).

Pelleted paper products are highly recommended for bedding material. Use of wood shavings is discouraged. If you decide to use wood shavings, use only aspen shavings. These are the safest for chinchillas.

• Do not use pine or cedar shavings in your pet's cage. Shavings smell nice and look pretty, but they can cause medical conditions such as itchy skin, respiratory problems, and liver problems.

• Avoid wood chips. The sharp pieces can injure your pet's eyes.

• Avoid sawdust bedding. It is irritating to the lungs, can plug a chinchilla's small nostrils, and can dry and damage its eyes.

No matter what type of bedding you select, purchase only products that are packaged and indicated for use as bedding material for caged pets. Shavings, straw, and hay that are sold for use in horse stalls or that are stored in open outdoor bins may be contaminated with undesirable material such as urine and germs from wild rodents. They can be a health risk for your chinchilla and may spread disease to your pet.

Always make sure that the bedding material you use is as dust free as possible. Bedding that contains a lot of dust, mold, and fine particles can be very irritating to the lungs and cause wheezing, sneezing, and other respiratory problems.

Cleanliness

Bedding material should be changed at least once a week. If there is more than one animal in a cage, bedding should be replaced more often, as necessary.

Chinchilla Housekeeping

Chinchillas are clean animals and virtually odorless. They enjoy a clean cage. They are miserable when their cage is dirty. Clean the cage at least once a week, more often if necessary. If you can smell the cage, then it is past time to clean it!

The cage and cage floor should be easy to clean, nonporous, and resistant to moisture, salts, and cleansers. You can make a good disinfectant solution by mixing 1 part bleach to 20 parts water. Rinse the cage well and allow it to dry before returning your pet to the cage.

Do not use cleaning products that contain phenolics, such as Lysol or Pine-Sol. These are toxic to chinchillas.

Be sure to rinse the cage floor pan well with clean water and allow it to dry before adding bedding. If possible, leave the cage floor pan out in the sunshine to dry. The ultraviolet rays from the sun will also help kill bacteria.

A corner litter box with a high back takes up less cage floor space and helps prevent urinating outside of the cage.

Chemical Signals

If chinchillas are so clean, why do they urinate and defecate in their dust baths?

Taking a dust bath is not just a way to keep fur clean. Many hystricomorph rodents (such as degus) take dust baths in community dusting areas. This way, all the animals share the same odor and are socially acceptable to each other. It is reasonable to assume that this may be another reason chinchillas take dust baths. Because urine contains several substances and hormones that rodents use as a form of communication, by urinating in their dust baths, rodents send chemical signals that may mark an area as their territory and that tell a lot about themselves, including their identification, when they are in estrus, or when they are ready for mating.

The sides of the floor pan should be 3 to 4 inches (8.5 to 11 cm) high to prevent bedding material from spilling out of the cage.

Bottles, Dishes, Hayracks, and Feeders

Fresh water should be available at all times. One chinchilla drinks 1 to 2 ounces (30 to 60 mL) of water every day. Make sure your pet has at least one pint (473 mL) of fresh, pure, clean drinking water available in a bottle at all times. Do not give your chinchilla water in a bowl. Your pet can tip and spill a bowl of water or contaminate it with urine and feces. Kits can drown in a bowl of water.

Attach a glass or plastic water bottle to the outside of the cage so your chin has more cage space available for a play area. If the bottle is plastic, make sure your pet cannot chew on it.

Check the bottle sipper tube daily to be sure it is working properly and is not plugged with food, debris, or bedding material. Bacteria grow and multiply in dirty sipper tubes and contaminate the water. Clean the sipper tube thoroughly each day with a round brush.

A hayrack is a good way to keep grass hay clean and fresh. A J-feeder works well for feeding pelleted foods because a chinchilla cannot contaminate its food by sitting in the feeder and defecating or urinating in it. J-feeders also make it difficult for the animal to dig or scatter food pellets and helps prevent food wastage. A broad-based or weighted dish made of chew-proof material that is safe for rodents (such as stainless steel or ceramic) is ideal for feeding small treats.

Hideaways and Tunnels

Every cage should contain at least one hideaway, preferably more. This can be as simple as a wooden nest box, a large flowerpot, or a PVC plumbing pipe. If the hideaway is made of wood, your pet will chew on it. PVC pipes are safe, cheap, easy to clean, and can be purchased at your local hardware store. They should be long enough and large enough in diameter that the animal can fit inside comfortably. PVC pipes can be hung near the top of the cage, freeing up cage floor space

Fresh water should be available at all times. Make sure your pet can reach the sipper tube and that it is not plugged.

and acting as a shelf as well as a hiding place. Your chinchilla will spend a lot of time resting and feeling secure in its hideaways. They provide the dark and quiet your pet would experience in an underground burrow. When your chin is tired of all the activity, light, or noise in its environment, it can retreat to a hideaway and relax. Hideaways reduce cage stress and are an absolute necessity for your pet's health and well-being.

Dust Baths—A Regular Ritual

Chinchillas are meticulously clean and virtually odorless. Their luxurious coats are plush and soft to touch. They require just some simple care on your part (see "Grooming") and regular dust baths.

In captivity, as in the wild, chinchillas keep their coats free of dirt and prevent natural oils from accu-

Chinchillas feel safe and secure in their hideaways.

with lids, designed especially for chinchillas, are available from pet stores or chinchilla suppliers. One style of dusting bin resembles a giant plastic jar. This keeps the spread of dust down to a minimum, yet allows you to watch your pet's antics as it delights in the dust. Although your chinchilla would use any shallow container large enough for it to fit in and roll about comfortably (such as a plastic or stainless steel bowl, ceramic crock, or small box), this is not recommended because of the amount of dust that your pet will disperse into the air.

Chinchilla coat care could not be any easier or any more fun! Just let your chinchilla take a dust bath at least twice a week and enjoy the show! Place the dust bath inside the cage and wait for the action! It will not take long. Your chin will quickly hop right in and roll around and around in the dust. It may jump in and out of the dust bath several times and stir up quite a cloud, so be sure the cage is in an area where dust will not bother you or anything in the house (such as computers and other sensitive electronics). An air filter in the room will help keep dust down and keep everyone—animals and humans—comfortable. Allow your chin ten to 15 minutes to enjoy its dust bath, and then remove the bath immediately before your pet can urinate or defecate in it.

On the Run! Exercise Wheels

An exercise wheel is a chinchilla necessity as well as a toy. Chinchillas

mulating and matting down the coat by rolling in clean dust. Dust baths also help keep the skin healthy.

Dusting powder specifically sold for chinchillas can be purchased from your local pet store or online from chinchilla suppliers through the Internet. Several brands are available, including Blue Cloud and Blue Sparkle Chinchilla Dust.

Place two cups of dusting powder in a dusting container. Dusting bins

A large tunnel tube makes a fun hiding place.

are very active animals that love to run. An exercise wheel provides a form of entertainment, social enrichment, and a way to maintain body condition. Your pet will run miles in its wheel and will use it every day. In fact, if your chinchilla is not interested in its wheel, this may be an early sign that it does not feel well.

Purchase an exercise wheel that is sturdy and large enough to accommodate your chinchilla: at least 18 inches (46 cm) in diameter for adults and 12 to 14 inches (30 to 36 cm) in diameter for youngsters. It should be no less than four inches (10 cm) and ideally 6 inches (15 cm) wide. The wheel should have a solid floor rather than rungs. A solid floor prevents foot sores and accidents (such as broken legs caused by

An exercise wheel is an absolute necessity. The wheel should be large enough that your pet can stretch out and run in it comfortably. Do not use wheels with rungs. They can cause injuries.

being caught in rungs). Wheels can be freestanding or attached to the cage wall. A freestanding wire wheel crowds a cage and takes up valuable floor space that could be better used as a play area. More important, freestanding wheels can be a potential danger if one animal is running in it and another one tries to jump on while the wheel is in motion. The second animal can become trapped between the support that runs the

Dustbaths are a necessity. They remove excess oils and keep your pet's coat clean and its skin healthy.

diameter of the wheel and the vertical bar of the wheel stand.

Attach the wheel to the side of the cage, or better yet, hang it from the top of the cage. By suspending the wheel, the potential for accidents is lessened and your pet will have more play area available on the cage floor.

If you have more than one animal housed together and enough space in the cage, consider buying an additional exercise wheel so that both animals can run at the same time. Chinchillas can be very possessive about their wheels and do not always like to share!

Remember that chinchillas, although active off and on during the day, are nocturnal and busiest at night. If you are a light sleeper, you may want to place your pet's cage somewhere in your home where the sounds of the running wheel will not disturb you. You may decide to give your chinchilla access to its exercise wheel during the daytime only. Your pet will then be more active during the day and you can sleep better at night.

Play It Safe! Toys for Your Chinchilla

Chinchillas are playful, curious animals. They are active year-round and do not hibernate. When housed together, they spend much of their recreational time playing and interacting with each other. Because of their social, inquisitive nature, chinchillas need a cage large enough for them to romp and socialize. They also need plenty of safe, interesting toys. Toys are a worthwhile investment in your little friend's happiness. Chinchillas love to play and explore, and you will love watching them!

Chinchillas constantly nibble and chew. Their teeth grow continually and must be worn down, so they need a steady supply of safe rodent chew toys, such as wooden sticks or branches. It is best to purchase safe rodent chew sticks from the pet store. However, if you decide to give your pet twigs and sticks, be certain that these materials do not have any sharp edges and that they do not come from any poisonous or potentially harmful plant or tree, such as cedar, cherry, oleander, plum, or redwood. Aspen wood makes excellent rodent chew sticks. Apple, birch, and maple are also suitable for chew sticks.

Never give your chinchilla painted or treated wood.

Chinchillas appreciate any objects or activities that make life more interesting. They love things they can climb over, push around, or scamper through. Toys that dangle or hang from the top of the cage are very popular. A simple ball (chew proof, please!) that can be pushed around the cage makes a great toy! Other favorite playthings include hiding places, nest boxes, platforms, large blocks, or flat rocks on which to sit. You can buy these items at your local pet store or make many of them yourself. For example, you can create inexpensive tunnels from PVC plumbing pipe from your local hardware store. PVC is safe for your pet, inexpensive, easy to clean, and reusable. You can also make wooden nest boxes and hiding places from untreated, nontoxic wood. Just keep in mind that whatever kinds of toys you give, your pet will chew on them! Be sure they are made of safe, nontoxic materials.

Often the simplest and cheapest things make the most interesting toys. For example, a simple shower curtain ring attached to the wall of the cage will provide your curious chin with hours of entertainment. A paper bag gives your pet a place to investigate, crawl into, and tear to pieces! It does not take much! Your pet's toy box collection is limited only by your imagination!

Chinchillas love a wide variety of chew toys. Make sure to give ones that are safe for pets, such as aspen wood.

Selecting the Perfect Spot

Finding just the right location for your pet's cage is important. You have to keep your companion's comfort in mind, as well as cleanliness and convenience. For example, some chinchillas position themselves in such a way when they urinate that they may spray outside of the cage, so do not place the cage close to a wall or the wall may stain.

Find a place that is out of direct sunlight. Even if the temperature within your home is comfortable, a cage placed in direct sunlight can heat up rapidly, especially cages with metal backs or sides.

Do not put the cage near a steamy bathroom where the humidity is too high or the air is damp. Do not put the cage close to wood stoves, fireplaces, or heating vents where the temperature can climb above the comfort level and your chinchilla could die from heatstroke.

Chinchillas are susceptible to respiratory problems, so make sure to place the cage in an area away from cold, drafts, and air-conditioning vents so your pet does not become chilled and develop pneumonia. Kits are even more sensitive than adults to temperature fluctuations and extremes.

Place your chin's home at a comfortable level for viewing and handling. Choose a spot where you can enjoy its activities and are able to reach in to catch it or feed it, clean the cage, change the water bottle, and replace the bedding, toys, and dust bin without having to bend over or stoop.

Finally, keep your companion's overall environment in mind. Chinchillas are sensitive and easily frightened by loud noises and sudden movements (especially movements from overhead). Do not place the cage near the family sound system speakers, television set, or slamming doors.

Chinchillas feel most secure when they can be on the lookout for dangers and for friends. Your chinchilla will want to know when you come home and where you are. Do not obstruct its view by blocking the cage with furniture and walls! Your pet wants to see what's going on!

Chapter Five

Feeding Your Chinchilla

Chinchillas love to eat—in fact, mealtime is one of their very favorite times of day! Of all the things you do for your pet, feeding it a nutritious, balanced diet ranks among the most important because *good health is not possible without good nutrition*. A quality diet is one of the best and simplest ways to make sure your chinchilla has a long life span, a beautiful coat, and fewer health problems (including less reproductive problems if you are planning on breeding and raising chinchillas). That's why it is so important to buy only the best and freshest food you can find. Never cut corners when it comes to feeding your chin a quality diet. Fortunately, good nutrition is very easy and inexpensive to provide.

Strictly Vegetarian

Chinchillas not only look different from most common pets, they *are* different! Their digestive system is long and delicate, and they have special nutritional needs. Unlike many rodents that are omnivorous and will eat almost anything to sur-

vive, chinchillas are strict vegetarians (herbivorous, eating plant materials only). Although not enough scientific research has been done yet to determine all of the specific nutritional requirements of chinchillas, many good chinchilla foods are available commercially that appear to cover all the bases and that have worked very well for chinchilla breeders and pet owners throughout the years.

Chinchilla Food Choices

Good nutrition plays an important role in your chinchilla's overall health. If your pet does not receive proper nutrition or a balanced diet, it can suffer from a variety of health problems, including premature death. The good news is that you have full control of your little friend's diet—and providing a diet that is not only nutritious and balanced but delicious as well is very easy!

Your chinchilla has special behavioral, anatomical, and biological considerations that influence its dietary needs. For example, its gastrointestinal tract is very sensitive and very long. It can be easily upset by a sudden change in diet or the wrong kinds

You can prevent problems by feeding a healthy, balanced diet from the day you acquire your chinchilla. Be consistent. If your pet is eating a good diet, do not change it unless there is an excellent reason to do so. If you must change the diet, change it gradually. A sudden dietary change can stress your chinchilla so much that it may develop severe gastrointestinal problems.

of foods. Bacteria in the gut also play an important role in how nutrients are absorbed. If you see your chinchilla eat its feces, do not be alarmed. This is called coprophagy (a fancy term for "eating feces"). Your pet is consuming cecotropes, a special kind of feces produced as a way to recycle needed nutrients, including B vitamins, vitamin K, and some minerals.

In addition, a chinchilla's teeth (incisors and molars) grow continuously throughout life. Roughage in the diet helps to keep the teeth ground down and prevents some dental problems. Good-quality grass hay is excellent and essential for this purpose and provides necessary roughage for digestion.

All mammals (except humans, nonhuman primates, guinea pigs, and some fruit bats) are able to synthesize their own vitamin C (ascorbic acid) and do not need it included in their diet. Vitamin C is a water-soluble vitamin that is excreted in the urine daily.

Chinchillas are distantly related to guinea pigs. Although research has not yet determined all of the specific needs of chinchillas, we know that guinea pigs require vitamin C in the diet and that chinchillas with gum and dental problems can benefit from additional vitamin C in the diet. So play it safe. Make sure vitamin C is included in your pet's diet. This can be done by purchasing *fresh* foods that contain vitamin C and by offering small fruit treats rich in vitamin C on occasion.

What to Feed

The ideal chinchilla diet is a correct balance of nutrients (proteins, fats, carbohydrates, vitamins, minerals, and water) fed in just the right amount for the animal's stage in life: growth, maintenance, reproduction, and age. Commercial chinchilla pellets, available from pet stores or feed stores, are ideal for pet chinchillas.

The correct balanced chinchilla diet formula ranges from 10 to 20 percent protein, 2 to 5 percent fat, and 15 to 35 percent bulk fiber, depending on the animal's individual needs. In order to cover all the nutritional bases, commercial feed companies have developed mixtures of balanced foods, produced in pellet form, specifically for chinchillas. So your part is simple. All you have to do is purchase a quality chinchilla food, *make sure it is fresh*, and feed it free choice (ad libitum) along with a handful of fresh timothy hay daily and a few supplements and treats

Feeding your pet a quality balanced diet is one of the most important and easiest things you can do to keep it healthy.

when needed, and your chinchilla should thrive. What could be easier?

Some quality chinchilla pellets include Mazuri Chinchilla Pellets, Purina Chinchilla Pellets, Oxbow Chinchilla Deluxe, and Hubbard's Tradition Chinchilla Pellets. These can be found through your local feed or pet store or online through the Internet.

Feed Only Fresh Food

Be sure the food you provide is fresh. Sometimes food is displayed in store windows in the front of the pet store. The food can get hot and lose its nutritional value. Buy only food that is fresh and stored in a cool, dry place.

Check the milling date on the food package to verify the shelf life of the product. If you cannot find a milling date, check for a statement that says "use before" and make note of the

date stamped on the package. If the food is old, the vitamins in the food will lose their potency and no longer be effective. This is especially true for vitamin C. Although standard laboratory recommendations are to provide food that is no older than six months (180 days) from the time of milling, you should definitely discard any food that is more than 90 days old from the time of milling. This is because once the food package has been opened and the food has been exposed to atmospheric conditions, vitamins begin to lose their potency. For example, vitamin C deteriorates very rapidly. In fact, 50 percent of the vitamin C efficacy in the feed is lost within six weeks of milling.

Do not buy food within six weeks of the expiration date. Buy only as much food as your chinchilla will eat in one month so you will not have to worry about food becoming too old

Laboratories

Chinchillas housed in laboratories are fed commercially formulated chinchilla pellets, up to 8 ounces (250 g) every day, depending on their needs. They are not supplemented with fruits, vegetables, or treats. Although it is unpleasant to think about, in most research institutions every laboratory chinchilla that dies must undergo a necropsy (autopsy for animals) to determine the cause of death or if any other problems were present. So if the animals had nutritional problems, these would be noted. Interestingly, laboratory chinchillas do very well on a simple diet of commercial chinchilla food without supplementation. Of course, this does not mean your cherished chinchilla has to eat such a spartan diet, but it does offer assurance that the commercial chinchilla foods appear to cover the nutritional bases well.

during storage. Do not add old food to new food in a container. If the food is old, discard it. Old food loses its nutritional value and the vitamins in the food lose potency. If you combine old and new food, there is no way to know what amount of the food has been stored the longest or how old it is, and you may end up feeding your pet stale food.

Be sure also to throw away any fines (pellets that have become finely ground and turned to dusty powder at the bottom of the feed container). This is old food that has no nutritional value and may grow fungi or mold.

To prolong freshness, you can freeze food that you will not be using immediately. However, the best way to make sure the food you feed is fresh is to buy small quantities at a time.

Always store your pet's food in a closed container in a cool, dark, dry, clean, well-ventilated place.

Food Pellets for Other Species?

Some chinchilla owners prefer to feed a combination of quality commercial guinea pig pellets (because they contain vitamin C), rabbit pellets (for fiber), and rodent pellets in an effort to cover all of the nutritional bases. There is not total agreement among veterinarians or chinchilla breeders as to whether a combination of pellets is the best diet to feed. Some researchers think that rabbit

Your chinchilla should have fresh hay available at all times, every day.

pellets may contain too much vitamin D or may be harmful to chinchillas. On the other hand, some veterinary authors support this dietary combination, and many chinchilla breeders report that their chinchillas do well when fed *high-quality* rabbit pellets. It is safest to feed a quality diet manufactured specifically for chinchillas when possible, unless you have first-hand information or experience that a certain pellet combination works well for chinchillas. For example, if you purchase your chinchilla from a breeder who has good success with a combination diet, continue to feed your chinchilla the diet the breeder uses and recommends.

No matter what type of pelleted diet you feed, all pellets should be the correct size, firmness, and consistency for chinchillas to manage. Chinchillas eat their food using their forepaws, so pellets should be long enough for them to grasp easily and firm enough not to crumble while they are being held.

Binders are substances used to bind pelleted food, to hold it together firmly. Binders include molasses or chemicals such as sodium bentonite. It has been suggested, but not confirmed by laboratory studies, that sodium bentonite may cause fecal impaction in rabbits. Check the label on your pet's food to determine what type of binder is used. If your pet suffers from gastrointestinal problems such as constipation or dry feces, consider avoiding products that use sodium bentonite as a binder.

Chinchillas love hay cubes. Be sure the cubes you feed are a good blend of hays and are not too rich in alfalfa.

How Much to Feed

Your chinchilla should, ideally, have food available at all times. Any spoiled, wasted, or contaminated food should be removed from the feeder daily.

Some people like to schedule mealtimes for their pets. It is better for a chinchilla to have food available at all times (also called free choice or *ad libitum*) and simply to schedule treats. However, if you prefer to feed your chinchilla on a schedule, bear in mind that a regular feeding schedule is very important and just as impor-

Chinchillas have tiny, dainty digits. They use these digits to hold their food, so be sure their food pellets and food are easy for them to grasp.

tant as what you feed and how much you feed. Chinchillas look forward to their food, and a change in schedule can upset their digestive tract. If you do not feed your pet free choice, be sure to feed it at least twice daily.

Your pet should receive at a minimum 2 tablespoons (30 mL) of chinchilla food each day. If your chinchilla is large, active, pregnant, lactating, stressed, or recovering from an illness, it will require much more food, so pay close attention not to underfeed your hungry companion.

The easiest, safest, and recommended feeding method is to have fresh food available at all times and to discard used food at the end of each day before you add new food to the feeder. This will prevent underfeeding. It will also prevent the accumulation of stale food, fine particles, and mold contamination.

Enough Food to Go Around

One of the best ways to be sure you are feeding your pet correctly is to talk to the chinchilla breeder from whom you purchased your chin and feed the same food it has been eating at the breeder's. Chinchilla breeders are knowledgeable and can recommend quality chinchilla foods available in your area.

The most accurate indicator of how well a diet meets your pet's needs is by close observation. If your chinchilla is in excellent health, is not too fat and not too thin, is bright and alert, has a good appetite, has a beautiful coat, loves to play, and has normal feces, then you can safely assume that you are feeding it correctly. *Feces are very important indicators of health!* Do not be misled into thinking your pet is the perfect weight simply by looking at it. All that fur can make your chinchilla look chunkier than it is! Feel its body carefully to make sure it is not underweight.

If you are housing two or more chinchillas together, make sure there is enough food for everyone. Some animals are greedier than others, and some are faster eaters. Some will eat more, and others will waste more. Provide enough food to go around and to compensate for wastage. Check your chins daily to be sure one or more is not becoming overweight or too thin. If they are, you may have to house them separately so you can monitor and control their individual food and water intake and make sure a health problem is not a factor.

The best way to know if your pet is maintaining (not gaining or losing) weight is to weigh it weekly. Purchasing a small scale to monitor your chinchilla's weight is a very wise investment.

Hay

Hay is an essential part of your chinchilla's daily diet and provides the necessary roughage for digestion. It also gives your pet something to do, especially when you are not around to keep it company. Chinchillas love to chew, and hay helps entertain as well as wear down teeth. *Make sure fresh hay is available at all times.*

The ideal hay for chinchillas is timothy hay. Whatever hay you purchase, it should smell fresh and sweet. Be sure it is not too moist and does not contain any dirt, debris, weeds, sticks, plastic, insects, mold, or mildew (usually present as a fine gray or black powder or has a burned appearance) and is not discolored, sharp, or brittle. When you purchase hay, you should receive quality hay, not straw (stems). Straw has no nutritional value, so check your purchase before you take it home.

It is safest to purchase hay that is specially packaged for small pets. Some good choices include Oxbow orchard grass and Oxbow oat hay. Do not buy "hay" designated for horse stalls (this would be straw) or hay that has been stored in open outdoor bins. Hay stored in outdoor

Observe your pet daily to be sure it is not too heavy or too thin.

bins may be contaminated with undesirable material, including mold, mildew, bird droppings, and urine, feces, and germs from wild rodents. All of these pose a great health risk for your chinchilla.

Types of hay include grass hays (timothy, Bermuda, fescue, Sudan, brome, buffalo, orchard grass); legume hays (clover, alfalfa, vetch); and grain hays (oats, barley). Grain hays should have the grain attached to it. Grains are easily contaminated by molds, so check the hays and grains closely before feeding them.

Timothy or other grass hay is excellent for your chinchilla's diet. Legume hays are, for the most part, too rich in protein and other nutrients and should be avoided. There is already an appropriate amount of legumes mixed into the commercially formulated pelleted food you feed your pet. Additional or excess legume hays can cause health prob-

Supplements

If you feed a quality commercial chinchilla diet and fresh hay daily, your chinchilla probably does not need any supplementation. However, if your pet is recovering from an illness, stressed, pregnant, lactating, or underweight, you can offer it a very small amount (no more than 1 teaspoon [5 mL] daily) of Calf Manna in a dish. (Calf Manna is available from your local feed store.) Do not mix the Calf Manna in the feeder with the chinchilla diet because your pet will dig out and waste its food pellets as it seeks out the much-preferred Calf Manna.

Nuts, Seeds, and Grains

You may feed your chinchilla a very small amount (not to exceed ½ to 1 teaspoon [2.5 to 5 mL] daily) of a mixture of oats, wheat, bran, flax, and barley as an alternative supplement. Do not feed corn; it is fattening and can cause skin allergies. Keep nuts to a minimum (one to two a week). They are very fattening.

Most chinchillas love sunflower seeds. Feed only shelled, raw, unsalted seeds. Limit them to one or two per day.

Feed nuts, seeds, and grains in a small dish, separate from the pellet feeder, so that your chinchilla does not dig out and waste the pellets as it searches for tastier tidbits.

lems, including gastrointestinal problems (diarrhea and bloat) and possibly hormonal imbalances (for example, from plant estrogens).

Some hay can be purchased in small blocks or cubes for convenience in feeding and storage. Although hay cubes may be more expensive than packaged, loose, or baled hay, cubes are not as messy, there is less wastage, and chinchillas love them. Hay cubes are also ideal for traveling with your pet because they are convenient to transport and feed.

Store your pet's hay in a clean, cool, dark, dry place, free of contaminants. Buy only a small amount of hay at a time so that the hay you feed is always fresh. Pick up soiled hay from the cage bottom daily and discard it.

Treats

Your chinchilla would eat as many treats as you would offer it, so it's up to you to use good judgment! Don't let your pet become overweight, no matter how much it begs! Limit treats to "healthy" treats only, such as a raw, unsalted, shelled sunflower seed or a small piece of dried fruit. *Limit treats to one or two small treats each day.* Limiting treats is hard because giving your bright-eyed, begging friend something special to eat is so much fun. But if you are not careful, you can kill your pet with kindness. *Too many treats lead to obesity, health problems, and a shortened life span.*

Raisins are a favorite chinchilla treat, but are they safe? Raisins (and grapes) have been reported to be toxic to some pets. For example, as little as seven raisins can kill a dog. So maybe we should think twice about feeding raisins and keep these toxicity findings in mind. Besides, raisins are high in sugar and can upset a chinchilla's gastrointestinal tract. Play it safe by selecting other types of treats, such as a dry shredded wheat. You can offer dried fruit occasionally to your pet as treats and vitamin C supplements. Acceptable dried fruits that you can give your chinchilla are cranberries, bananas, berries, apples, apricots, figs, pears, and peaches (the last three are especially rich in vitamin C). Whatever fruit you give, remember that fruits are high in sugar content, so limit intake to one small piece of dried fruit per day or every other day.

Dietary Guidelines

Feeding your chinchilla a nutritional, healthy diet is easy if you follow some basic guidelines.

1. Feed your pet a quality commercial chinchilla food.
2. Make sure fresh grass hay is available at all times.
3. Limit the amount of treats daily.
4. Do not feed any foods that are not suitable for chinchillas: foods rich in sugar or fats, sticky foods, and candies—all can cause health problems.

Check to be sure the dried fruit products do not contain sulfites. Sulfites are harmful to chinchillas. Consider purchasing a food dehydrator to make wholesome, preservative-free treats for your chin (and for yourself).

Vegetables

You do not need to feed your chinchilla vegetables if it is receiving a quality chinchilla diet. Some vegetables, such as onions, can be harmful to your pet. Many vegetables cause excessive gas production and could lead to bloat. Lettuce can cause diarrhea and may contain the toxin laudanum. Spinach and beet tops are rich in oxalates that can cause urinary tract problems. The green parts of potatoes contain solanine, a poison. In addition, vegetables may be contaminated with pesticides, parasites, or bacteria (such as *Yersinia* and *Salmonella*).

Whenever you start adding other food types to your pet's diet, you upset the balance of the commercial

Helpful Feeding Guidelines

Food	Amount to Feed	Advantages
Pelleted commercial chinchilla food	Available at all times (free choice, *ad libitum*) or two meals daily. Feed no less than 1 tablespoon (15 mL) of pellets per meal. Increase food intake for growing, pregnant, lactating, stressed, or debilitated animals	Convenience, nutritionally balanced
Hay (loose or in cubes)	Available at all times (free choice, *ad libitum*)	Helps wear down teeth and provide roughage; keeps pet entertained
Treats	One very small piece of dried fruit daily and one raw, unsalted, shelled sunflower seed daily	Optional source of vitamin C
Shredded wheat	Small piece	Provides roughage; may help control diarrhea

diet. For example, if you are feeding quality chinchilla pellets and hay (a balanced, nutritious diet) and start to add other ingredients, the foods that you add disrupt the balance of proteins, carbohydrates, fats, minerals, vitamins, and other nutrients in your pet's overall diet.

Many chinchilla owners say their pets like to eat vegetables. What is not to like about fresh veggies? Just because chins like them does not mean they are good for them! Chinchillas all have various discriminating tastes, and they all love food. At issue is not whether chinchillas like vegetables or not but rather how much the addition of different foods interferes with the nutritional balance of the animal's overall food intake. In other words, if your pet is eating a quality chinchilla diet, vegetables do not need to be added to the diet.

Mineral Salt Blocks and Stones

Mineral salt blocks can be beneficial for chinchillas, although not all chinchillas will use them. Salt blocks come in different colors. Pink and red are mineral salt blocks and may contain selenium; yellow contains sulfur; white is plain salt. Any color is safe for chinchillas. Red salt blocks are usually preferred by chinchilla breeders.

If the ingredients for your pet's food are grown in an area that is deficient in certain minerals, a mineral salt block can offset what is lacking in the feed. For example,

Quality varies according to manufacturer, ingredients, and location where ingredients are grown

Must be fresh! Can be contaminated with disease-causing organisms (from wild rodents or mold), causing allergy, pneumonia, or infection; is messy

Excess treats can cause obesity and health problems

Dehydrating

If you feed your chinchilla a quality diet, you do not have to give it supplements. Limit treats and feed healthy treats only.

some agricultural soils are low in selenium. A deficiency in dietary selenium can cause muscle and nervous system problems. By supplementing with a selenium mineral salt block, health problems may be prevented. To learn more about the type of mineral salt block you should give your pet, consult your veterinarian and the local feed store where you buy your chinchilla food and hay.

Some salt blocks contain larvicides (chemicals to kill insect larvae). These salt blocks are usually quite large and are for use in large animal species (horses, cattle). They are toxic to chinchillas, so *be sure that the salt block you give your pet is free of larvicides.*

Mineral stones containing calcium are available in pet stores.

Feeders and Hayracks

You can prevent some food wastage by purchasing special feeders (hoppers), such as J-shaped feeders, to use for feeding pellets. J-shaped feeders attach to the outside of the cage and do not take up cage floor space. It is also difficult to spill food out of a J-shaped feeder.

Hayracks should be used for feeding hay. Hayracks help keep hay clean by keeping it off the cage floor. They also make eating hay more interesting, as the chinchilla has to reach, pull, and work somewhat to get the hay out of the rack.

Harmful Foods

Do not feed your chinchilla the green parts of potatoes or potato eyes as these contain a poison called solanine. Do not feed cooked or processed foods (they may be lacking in vitamins or contain food additives and preservatives). Do not feed chocolate (which contains theobromine, a product similar to caffeine) or other candies. If you are not sure about the safety or nutritional benefit of any food type, simply do not feed it to your pet.

Water

Researchers have reported that chinchillas in the wild do not appear to drink water. They also report that chinchillas in the wild have a choice of up to 24 plant species to eat, including grasses, herbs, and moisture-filled succulents. In captivity, chinchillas do not have such a varied and moist diet and must drink water to survive. In fact, one chinchilla drinks 1 to 2 ounces (30 to 60 mL) daily when fed a regular dry diet of pellets and hay.

Depending upon where you live, contents of city or well water may vary and could contain additives such as chlorine, chloramine, and fluorine; high levels of undesirable elements such as arsenic; or low levels of bacteria. The best water you can give your chinchilla is the same drinking water you filter or buy for yourself. Do not give your chin distilled, demineralized, or deionized water. Just like humans, animals require natural minerals found in spring water. Do not give your pet water that has been treated by a water softener. It is too high in sodium.

Commercial bottled drinking water is an inexpensive and safe way to ensure the health of your pet.

Chinchillas should have fresh water available at all times. Use water bottles. Dishes are not recommended because water can be spilled and contaminated and because young chinchillas can drown in a small, shallow water dish.

Provide at least 1 pint (473 mL) of fresh, pure, clean drinking water for each chinchilla at all times. Water is especially important because your pet's diet is dry pellets and dry hay. *A dry diet increases thirst and the need for water.*

Water consumption depends on health, condition, age, and environmental conditions. It is also greatly influenced by activity level and reproductive cycle. If your chinchilla is pregnant or nursing kits, it can easily drink more than twice the amount of water it usually does. Room temperature and humidity also affect how much water your pet consumes. Animals housed in a warm, dry room will drink more than those in cooler, more humid environments.

Always provide more water than your chinchilla normally drinks. If you are housing several animals together, be sure the water supply is sufficient to give the animals all the water they will need plus a little extra and make

Prevent obesity by feeding a balanced diet and limiting treats. Your chin will live a longer, healthier life!

sure the sipper tube is within the animals' reach.

Check the sipper tube daily to be certain it is functioning properly and is not plugged. Closely watch the water level in the bottle to be sure your pet is drinking. Sipper tubes plugged with bedding material or debris have been responsible for many pet deaths caused by thirst and dehydration.

If you have kits, they should also have access to the sipper tube. Although their mother will nurse them for six to eight weeks, they will begin to drink water and eat solid food within a week of birth. Lower the water bottle so that the sipper tube is 1 to 2 inches (2.5 to 5 cm) above the cage floor, within reach of the kits. Make sure it is not so low that it comes in contact with the cage bedding. If this happens, the sipper tube can either become plugged or the water may completely wick out into the bedding material. Bacteria rapidly

multiply in sipper tubes plugged with debris, causing water contamination.

Clean your chinchilla's dishes, bottles, and sipper tubes with a mild detergent, like the one you use for your own dishes. Rinse them thoroughly, and completely remove all traces of the detergent. You can also soak the bottle and sipper tube for a few minutes in mildly chlorinated water and then rinse them thoroughly, several times. If you prefer, you can use boiling water to rinse the water bottle and soak the sipper tube. When the water bottle and sipper tube are rinsed well and completely cooled, fill the water bottle with commercial bottled drinking water sold for human consumption.

Baby Chin Safety

Baby chinchillas can drown in a small bowl of water. Do not give your kits a water dish. Give them water using bottles and sipper tubes only.

Chapter Six

Your Chinchilla Comes Home

The big day has arrived! You have found a wonderful chinchilla, and the chemistry between you and your new pet is perfect! Now it's time to bring it home. Everything has to be ready and just right for the new arrival, so make sure nothing has been overlooked.

Selecting a Veterinarian

Chinchillas are fun pets that do very well with good care and nutrition, spacious housing, and lots of attention. Just in case your pet has a problem or is sick or injured, it will need to be seen by a veterinarian for an examination and possible treatment. Early diagnosis and treatment of health problems is one of the most important keys to chinchilla longevity. If you own several chins and one of them is sick, it is important to determine the cause of illness to be sure that the problem is not contagious to you or your other pets.

Have everything prepared in your pet's cage before you bring it home. And don't forget the chew sticks.

Many veterinarians specialize in exotic animals or have a special interest and expertise in less-common pets. Chinchillas' needs differ from those of larger companion animals and other rodent pets. They are also sensitive to certain products and medications used for treating other animal species.

Plan ahead. Contact veterinarians *before* your pet needs veterinary care. This gives you an opportunity to introduce yourself as a possible future client and meet the veterinarians in your area who are knowledgeable in chinchilla care. *Decide in advance* where you would take your chin if it were sick. That way you will not be burdened with finding a veterinarian and making such an important decision during an emergency situation.

You and your veterinarian are a team. You will share responsibility for your little friend's health throughout its long life. Naturally, you will be as particular about choosing a veterinarian as you are about selecting your own doctor. Fortunately, there is no shortage of excellent veterinarians, but how do you find the veteri-

Your chinchilla will appreciate a warm, comfortable, cozy spot.

narian that is right for you and your companion?

Here are some guidelines to help you in the selection process:

• Ask satisfied chinchilla owners and chinchilla club members which veterinarians they recommend in your area. Word of mouth is one of the best ways to find a veterinarian.

• Find a veterinarian who knows a lot about chinchillas, who has worked with them, and who appreciates them as much as you do. Many veterinarians advertise in telephone directories, but the size or style of an advertisement is not an indicator of the best match for your pet's special needs.

• Consider convenience. What are the doctors' office hours, schedule, and availability? Is the doctor available on weekends and holidays or in case of emergency? How close is the veterinary clinic or hospital? Will you be able to travel there quickly in the event of an emergency?

• What are the fees for services? Most veterinarians provide a price estimate for anticipated services and expect payment when service is rendered. Ask what types of payment methods are available.

• Make an appointment to tour the veterinary hospital facilities. Examine all of the hospital during your visit, and pay attention to the clinic's cleanliness and odors.

Remember!
Don't forget to make a list of all the questions and topics you want to discuss with your veterinarian. That way you won't forget to ask something important and you can make the most of every minute of your consultation.

The first veterinary visit should take place within 48 hours of purchasing your pet. Most breeders and pet stores offer a health guarantee, ranging from 48 hours to one week, depending on the seller. Take advantage of this opportunity to take your chin to a veterinarian for a health checkup. If, during the health guarantee period, your pet has a problem or becomes ill, you can return it for a full reimbursement if you desire or begin medical treatment if necessary.

Whenever you take your chin to the veterinarian, be sure to ask any questions you have about your new pet. Do not be shy. It is an ideal time to discuss your chin's special needs and the breeder's or pet store's recommendations, and to plan a complete health care program. Always discuss nutrition, and weigh your chinchilla. Your veterinarian will make assessments and keep a record of your pet's health. If there are any changes in the future, a comparison can be made that will be helpful in determining the progression or improvement of your pet's condition at that time.

Preparing for the Trip Home

You already have everything you need for your new pet ready and waiting: a spacious cage in a great location, nutritious food manufactured specifically for chinchillas, water bottles, dishes, hayracks, dust bin, exercise wheel, toys, and hideaways. Have your chinchilla's chambers all set up in advance so when you get home you can simply transfer the animal directly into its new environment. That way, it will not have to wait, confused and uneasy, in the travel cage while you get everything ready.

Buy a comfortable carrying kennel or travel cage to transport your pet— one that is escape proof and well ventilated. A small flight kennel, like the ones designed for cats or ferrets, will work well and can later serve as a hideaway if there is space for it within the cage.

Cover the carrying kennel with a light towel to block out some of the loud sounds and bright lights that might frighten your little traveler while it is being transported. Just be sure there is plenty of ventilation and air in the kennel.

Be sure to ask the breeder or pet store what brand of chinchilla pellets your new acquisition has been eating. Buy the same kind to feed your chin so it will not suffer the stress of a change in diet.

It's best to take your pet straight home from the breeder's or pet store. If you do need to stop for any reason, *remember never to leave your pet in a parked car on a warm day, even for a few minutes*. The temperature inside of a car, even with the windows cracked open and parked in the shade, can quickly soar past 120°F (49°C) within a few minutes. That is much too hot for any animal to survive, and chinchillas are very sensitive to heat. A chinchilla left in a car can die of heatstroke in a very short time.

The Great Escape: Preventing Chinchilla Casualties

Chinchillas are excellent escape artists! Before you bring your pet home, go through your house thoroughly several times, and look for any possible hazards a curious chin could encounter if it were to make the great escape. Look for any spaces or holes that it could slip through. You might not think of it that way, but your house can be a very dangerous place for your pet. Let us take a look at some of the many accidents waiting to happen in your home. That way you can prevent chinchilla casualties!

Rodent Traps and Poisons

As an animal lover, you probably do not have any rodent traps or poison around your home or garage. If

you do, though, remove them now! They are as deadly for your pet as they are for wild rodents.

Household Chemicals

Chinchillas love to explore and are very interested in everything. Make sure your chin does not get into a cabinet that contains household products such as cleaning agents, bug sprays, paints, fertilizers, pesticide baits, and other poisonous chemicals. All of these substances are extremely dangerous and potentially deadly for your pet. Chinchillas love to chew on anything wooden, including walls and baseboards. Some of these might be coated with toxic or lead-based paint.

Electrical Shock

If your chin escapes in the house, unplug and remove any electrical cords that may be within its reach. Your pet could cause a fire or die from electrocution if it chews on live electrical cords and wires.

Check the Laundry!

Before you do the laundry, check any piles of clothing you have lying on the floor so that you do not accidentally toss your pet into the washer with the laundry. It is not a likely accident for an adult chinchilla, but it could happen to an escaped baby chin, especially one that has

Your home can be a hazard for your chinchilla if it escapes. Close all cabinet doors and remove all poisons, rodent traps, chemicals, and toxic plants from your pet's reach.

hidden and is dozing snuggly in a soft pile of clothes. As crazy as it sounds, laundry and dryer accidents are not unusual.

Pets

Other pets in the house can be a serious threat to your chinchilla. No matter how gentle your dog, cat, or ferret is with you, they quickly regain instincts to hunt or kill small prey, especially when stimulated by the sight of an animal trying to flee. A fatal accident can take place in a split second. If your chinchilla escapes and finds a safe hiding place, put your other pets in a secure place where they cannot hurt it, and then capture your chinchilla as soon as possible and put it safely in its cage.

Outside Doors

Make sure all doors to the outside or the garage are closed. If your chinchilla escapes to the garage, it will be exposed to additional hazards and poisons. For example, it might find a few drops of antifreeze (ethylene glycol) on the garage floor. Antifreeze has a sweet taste that appeals to animals but is a deadly poison that causes kidney failure in a very short time. (Nontoxic antifreeze products are now available.)

If your pet escapes to the outdoors, you will never be fast enough to catch it as it speeds and leaps

A chin on the loose is a chin in danger. Make sure to securely fasten the cage door!

away—and it will be virtually impossible ever to find. Once outside, your pet has little chance of survival. A chinchilla is no match for the dangers of automobiles, neighborhood pets, wild animals, predator birds, and harsh weather conditions.

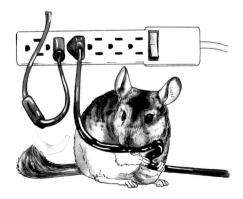

If your chinchilla escapes, it can chew on electrical cords and suffer electrical shock and possibly cause a fire. Immediately unplug all cords in your home until you find your pet.

Poisonous Plants

While your little herbivore is on the loose it may get hungry. What could be more appetizing than something green to eat? Unfortunately, many household and garden plants are poisonous, so be sure to remove any plants (as well as fertilizers and pesticides) that could make your chinchilla sick.

Crushing Injuries

Once you have an escapee in the house, everyone must pay close attention to where they step. Your chinchilla can dart underfoot in a heartbeat and could be tripped over or stepped on. Be careful where you step and where you sit down!

Capturing Your Chinchilla

If your chinchilla is loose in the house, you will probably hear it as it vocalizes (it may even call to you), gets into mischief, tears papers, and runs about, leaps, and explores. Do not try to catch your pet by chasing it all around the house. Chasing your pet will stress it and cause it to shed large amounts of its coat. Your chinchilla could also break a limb as it bounces and ricochets off objects and walls. Worse yet, if the animal is extremely panic stricken, chasing it around might stress it so much it could die. So easy does it!

The first thing to do is close all doors leading to the outside. Then, if

Common Poisonous Plants

Aconite
Amaryllis
American holly
American nightshade
Angel's trumpet
Azalea
Bird of paradise
Birdseye primrose
Blue cardinal flower (lobelia)
Buttercup (ranunculus)
Crocus
Chrysanthemum
Daffodil
Daily
Foxglove (digitalis)
Hydrangea
Iris
Lily (several species of lily)
Lupine
Mistletoe
Monkshood
Oleander
Onion
Philodendron
Poinsettia
Rhododendron
Tulip
Wolfsbane
Yew

your pet is in a room that can be shut off, enclose it in that limited area. Next try sitting quietly on the floor with one of your chin's favorite treats. Be very still and very patient. If your chin is very tame and recognizes you or is closely bonded to you, it will eventually come out of hiding to see what you have brought it. Let it have the treat so it will trust you in the future, and then gently scoop your pet up in both hands and hold on to it securely but not tightly.

When Children Assist

Chinchillas are great at escaping and children are gifted at finding things! So if children in the family are helping you look for your escapee, take advantage of their assistance, but remind them not to touch the animal when they find it because:

- A frightened chinchilla will not hesitate to bite.
- Chinchilla teeth can inflict serious bite wounds.
- If mishandled, the chinchilla could suffer a break or fracture, especially of the hind limbs.
- A child might unintentionally frighten your pet away before you can capture it.

Do not try to catch your chinchilla by grabbing at its fur. The fur will easily slip out. This is a defense mechanism called fur slip that makes it possible for a chinchilla to escape danger. However, it ruins the coat.

If your chinchilla is less manageable, not well socialized, or very flighty, you will need to use something to catch your pet without injuring it. Place a low-sided box in the center of the room, and place a treat inside of it. Or, you can put dust in the box to invite your chin to take a dust bath. Then sit back and wait. Your pet will come out of hiding to explore and is likely to jump into the box. You can then quickly throw a towel or sheet over the box to cover it while you transport your pet back to

A tightly woven fishing net can be very useful in capturing a frightened, flighty, hard-to-catch chinchilla.

its cage. If you do not have a suitable box, you can also try tossing a sheet or towel directly over the animal and rolling it up gently in the material to quickly transfer it to its home. Be careful when you do this. Do not crush or squeeze.

You can also try to catch your pet by simply shutting all the doors to the outside and leaving the cage door wide open, making a little trail of treats leading to the cage entry and baiting the inside of the cage with a favorite treat. Remember that chinchillas are philopatric and like to return home—when they know where it is! Turn down the lights and be very quiet so your pet will calm down after the excitement of its unauthorized free run of the house.

Another option is to purchase a small humane trap, such as a Havahart trap, at the local pet shop or feed store, or you may be able to rent or borrow one from your local animal shelter or veterinarian. (If you rent a trap, disinfect in thoroughly before you use it. It may have been

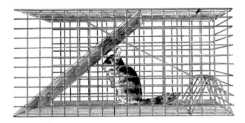

A humane trap, such as a Havahart trap, may be necessary to capture your chinchilla if it escapes. Be sure to check the trap several times a day.

used to trap sick or wild animals and could have germs on it that are dangerous to your chinchilla.) Trapping is a last-resort method for catching your pet because it might panic when it is trapped and ricochet inside of the trap and injure itself. It may also shed a lot of fur due to stress.

Bait the trap with your pet's favorite treat, and place it in an easily

accessible and quiet area. You are most likely to catch your pet during the evening when it is most active. Check your traps several times a day. By the time you catch your chin, it might be hungry and thirsty and very stressed. As a safety precaution, a tightly woven fish net is a good investment for catching runaway chins.

Whatever method you use to capture your pet, be gentle so you do not hurt it!

How to Hold and Restrain a Chinchilla

If your chinchilla loves to cuddle, you are very lucky! This kind of animal is quick to greet you when you approach its cage and eager to come out and visit. It is also easier to hold and handle. All you have to do is pick it up carefully and gently, using both hands as a scoop, and make sure it does not squirm loose or fall. Cuddling it is that simple!

To pick up a kit properly, cup both of your hands together and scoop the baby up under the rump and into the palms of your hands. Close your hands firmly, but not tightly, around the baby. You can also hold the kit with one hand, with your thumb and fingers gently grasping it around the belly. Be very careful not to hold or squeeze too tightly around the chest

If your pet escapes, dim the lights, close the doors, and be quiet and patient. Try to lure your chin with treats.

because you can accidentally damage the fragile tissues of the lungs. Hold your pet close against your chest with both hands to prevent it from falling.

An adult chinchilla can be held or restrained by holding the base of the tail (the part closest to the animal's body) and allowing the animal to rest its body on your forearm. Always hold onto the tail in case your pet is suddenly startled or decides to jump.

You can also lift your pet up by the base of its tail to move or reposition it quickly. Always hold on to the base of the tail only and never grab the tip of the tail. Holding, grabbing, or grasping a chinchilla by the tip of the tail can cause the tail to break or come off! This is a defense mechanism that allows the chinchilla to break lose and escape from predators. Unfortunately, the chinchilla loses its tail in the process, and the tail will not grow back.

Pregnant chinchillas must be lifted and held gently, with extreme care not to squeeze or crush the belly. Ideally the mother-to-be should be picked up by cupping two hands to support the extraheavy body and prevent struggling. *Never press on the abdomen or chest. Be gentle!*

Alternatively, a pregnant chinchilla can be grasped carefully with one hand and her rump supported with the other hand. This method can

result in hair loss (hair slip), so be very careful.

If your pet squirms and is difficult to hold, talk to it in a calm, soothing voice until it stops wriggling. One way to calm your pet is to offer it a small treat. Chinchillas can sometimes be distracted and reassured by a tasty morsel. Whatever you do, do not let your chinchilla drop or fall. When chinchillas are dropped, they almost always are seriously injured. Limbs, feet, and backs can be broken by falling or dropping even a short distance.

The Congenial Chinchilla

The more time you spend with your pet, the more sociable it will be. It will quickly learn to recognize you, bond to you, and demand attention from you. It will even greet you when you come home.

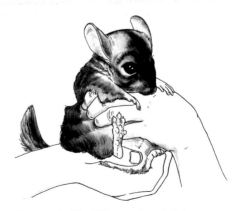

Pregnant chinchillas must be held carefully with both hands. One hand should be used to support the rump.

All that fur makes a chinchilla look bigger than it really is! Chinchillas can squeeze into the smallest of spaces. That is why they are such great escape artists!

Your plush-coated pet, with the endearing appearance, can be very sociable and quite entertaining. It does not annoy the neighbors, and it makes a wonderful, affectionate, cuddly companion. You cannot ask for anything more! So do not be disappointed if your chinchilla does not always do what you want it to do or if it fails to understand you. It will not come to you dependably when called, and it will not come out of, or go back into, its cage on command. Chinchillas are independent thinkers and like to do as they please! They also cannot be disciplined because

they do not know what they did wrong. *A chinchilla should never be punished in any way. Never strike or hit a chinchilla.*

Chinchillas respond to loving care but lose trust in their owners if treated unkindly.

Remember, a chinchilla is unique. It is not like a dog, cat, or any other rodent, for that matter. That is part of its beauty and mystique and one of the many reasons you wanted a chinchilla in the first place, right? So treat your pet gently and with compassion and understanding. In return it will trust you and be an affectionate friend.

Chapter Seven

Understanding Your Chinchilla

Our knowledge of chinchilla behavior is based on what we see at home and in research laboratories and what we read in the literature about chinchillas in the wild. Because wild chinchillas are now virtually nonexistent, most of our information comes from captive animals. We study, analyze, and make comparisons. We extrapolate and contemplate. However, we do not always have to observe a behavior to know something about it. For example, we know that wild chinchillas did not dig and that our pet chinchillas are not truly diggers. A look at chinchilla anatomy gives us some reasons why: chinchillas are not equipped with long, strong nails and powerful front limbs necessary for digging deep burrows in rocky terrain.

By studying animal behavior in the wild and in captivity and by taking into consideration the environment in which they evolved as well as their physical attributes and abilities, we can better understand their behaviors. For example, the facts that chinchillas are prey animals that need protective shelter but are not powerful diggers help explain why chin-

chillas prefer to live in rock crevices or in burrows already created and abandoned by other animals. We see the same characteristics in our small companions. They do not dig. Although they enjoy hideaways, they will not tunnel and create their own hiding places. We have to provide them.

By studying our pets' behaviors, we can make some reasonable assumptions about how chinchillas lived in the wild thousands of years ago, how that relates to their behavior today, why they do the things they do, and how we can take better care of them. The chinchilla's behaviors and ways of communicating reflect millions of years of ancestral development coupled with recent domestication—an interesting combination that makes for interesting observations!

The Social Chinchilla

The chinchilla's success as a house pet is due in large part to its highly social behavior. The more sociable an animal is, the more appealing it is as a pet. Social relations are important to chinchilla community living, too!

Chinchillas do best when housed in small family units or same-sex compatible pairs that have known each other from birth or from a very early age. They will develop a hierarchy (or pecking order) so that one animal is usually dominant. This alpha animal is usually a female. She can be very aggressive to males, even during breeding. Males will also fight with each other, especially if they are housed with females. Fights can be very serious and can even result in death.

Baby chinchillas have the best of all worlds. They follow their parents about, and their father is usually not only tolerant of them but friendly toward them. He will sit with them and their mother and be very protective. When they are not following the adults, the kits are playing with one another and get along well together almost all of the time.

When new individuals are introduced, they quickly begin to investigate each other. They cautiously approach and sniff. If the animals are not compatible, the dominant one will attack the newcomer.

Compatible chinchillas enjoy each other's companionship. They like to crowd close together to observe, to nap, or to take turns keeping guard. They are reasonable about sharing food and toys as well, except perhaps the exercise wheel, which is a highly prized possession!

Chinchilla Behavior

Knowing when your chinchilla feels happy, comfortable, and secure is easy. Its sense of well-being is contagious when it plays, runs in its wheel, takes dust baths, leaps, hops, grooms, naps, and snacks. All of these activities are signs of a happy, healthy chin.

Just like people, chinchillas have a variety of behaviors and act differently depending on their circumstances. The following describes some basic chinchilla behaviors to help you learn how to interpret your pet's moods and attitudes.

Aggressive behavior: Females can be very aggressive, especially toward males. Fighting can also take place between noncompatible females and noncompatible males.

Treat your chinchilla kindly and it will be an affectionate friend.

Chinchillas are naturally inquisitive and will investigate any place or thing they find.

Aggression is accompanied by threatening vocalizations.

Play behavior: Sometimes you will see your chin run through an entire repertoire of play behavior consisting of jumps, head shaking and hopping, bucking, cavorting, body twisting, and running. This play behavior is known among scientists as *frisky hops.* Although the term frisky hops does not sound like scientific terminology, it accurately describes this play behavior, which is seen most often among young animals. Frisky hops is considered to be an evolutionary form of antipredator flight play, providing a way for kits to practice movements that would allow them to escape from predators when they are adults. Play behavior is seen frequently among littermates.

Curiosity and interest: Chinchillas are interested in and curious about everything! An inquisitive chin will approach and investigate any new object you give it. Of course, it will always be just cautious enough that it can take off at a run if it feels threatened.

Fear: A chinchilla responds to fear by flight. This means that it will bolt and run away as fast as it can. This can result in accidents and injuries if your pet ricochets off walls and objects in the process. A frightened chinchilla may bite if it feels it is seriously threatened and there is no way to escape. If your pet is startled, return it to its cage, dim the lights, keep sounds to a minimum, and allow time for your pet to calm down before you handle it again.

Hair Pulling, "Barbering"

Chinchillas may pull out the fur of their cage mates. This type of behavior is usually seen in overcrowded conditions or stressful environments. It can become serious and develop into a form of aggression, with subordinate animals suffering the most.

Chinchillas Communicate in Many Ways
- Body language or visual cues
- Sense of touch or tactile communication
- Sense of smell and olfactory signals
- Voice signals or vocalizations

Chinchilla Body Language

	Behavior	Situation
Relaxed	Resting, eyes open, stretched out, lying down, or sitting comfortably	Usually resting in home cage or familiar area
Hops, chasing, body twisting, running	Play	Friendly encounter
Frightened	Hunched up, usually in a corner, may vocalize by "eek eek" or growling or snarling, tries to escape by racing about and bouncing off surfaces	Strangers, predators, introduction of a dominant and noncompatible animal into the cage, loud sounds, sudden movements
Threatened	Chinchillas (especially females) may stand up on hind limbs and spray urine at a perceived threat, whether animal or human!	Frightened, threatened, cornered, captured

Hair pulling (sometimes called *barbering*) can quickly ruin a beautiful coat. It can also lead to gastrointestinal obstruction from the formation of fur balls. If you see your pet pulling on another's fur or behaving in an unfriendly manner, remove the subordinate animals or give your pets more space. You can easily identify your underdogs. They are the ones with bald spots or areas of thinning hair. The dominant animals usually have no signs of hair loss.

Mutual Grooming

Tactile contact (touch) is an important and common part of social interactions. Compatible adult males and females will groom each other for up to ten or 15 minutes at a time. A chinchilla's way of asking to be groomed is by presenting its throat or nudging its forehead under the chin of its cage mate.

Chinchilla Communication

Chinchillas rely on their senses of sight, hearing, smell, and touch to communicate with one another, recognize their owners, identify other animals, and avoid predators.

Body Language

Your pet's body language is easy to recognize. Once you learn to inter-

Meaning	Function
Comfortable in environment, safe, and secure	Resting
Friendly, social interactions, especially among kits	Play, possibly to practice movements necessary to escape predators
Animal is frightened, feels insecure, and may panic	Survival, attempt to escape or defend itself
Frightened or feeling threatened	Self-defense

pret it, you will have no problem knowing when your pet is happy, feels threatened, is acting aggressively, is displaying mating behavior, or is playing.

Tactile and Olfactory Communication

Compatible chinchillas enjoy sitting close together. They actively seek each other's company and contact (tactile communication). This close body contact may be a way to exchange olfactory (scent) information and individual identification. The animals also likely derive comfort and a sense of security by being together. By crowding together, chins with established friendly rela-

tionships keep each other company and share warmth and the same body scents.

Make sure your chinchillas are compatible before you house them together. Females can be very aggressive toward males.

Chinchilla Vocalizations

Sound	Activity
Coos	These calls are similar to the sound of a dove's cooing and are made between males and females around the time of breeding
Chirp	Call made between mother and kits
Cry or squeal	This is a loud cry or shriek, almost like the scream of an injured rabbit, made when the chinchilla is extremely frightened or seized
Eek eek	Distress cry made when frightened, seized, or injured
Nyak nyak	Call made by isolated males, meaning not yet fully understood, considered one method for the animal to announce its presence or arousal
Growl	Sound made to threaten another chinchilla or a predator (if cornered and unable to escape)
Snarl	Sound made before or after an attack
Teeth chattering	May occur when threatened, when in pain, or in some cases, when content

When frightened or feeling threatened, a chinchilla may release a foul odor from its anal glands.

Vocalization

Chinchillas produce a variety of sounds (vocalizations) that signal their moods, although researchers do not yet know what they all mean. Chinchillas have keen hearing and are very sensitive to loud noises and are easily frightened by them. The following is a description of a few of the main sounds you will learn to recognize when your pet communicates.

Coos: These dovelike sounds are made between males and females at the time of courtship and breeding.

Chirps: Mother and baby chinchillas make soft calls to each other that sound like little birds chirping.

Eek eek: This is a loud, high-pitched noise. You will have no doubt about this sound when you hear it. It is the sound a chinchilla makes when it is injured, in pain, frightened, or captured.

Growls and snarls: Chinchillas do not growl or snarl often, but the sounds are easy to recognize, deep, and guttural. A chinchilla may growl if it feels threatened or is acting aggressively.

Screams, cries, and shrieks: These sounds are similar to those made by an injured rabbit and are made when a chinchilla is very frightened, captured, or injured.

Tooth chatter: Chinchillas chatter their teeth when they feel frightened. However, some tooth chatter has been associated with happy anticipation of a treat or a sign of satisfaction. Depending on the circumstances, you will know the difference when you hear it.

Nyak nyak: This repetitive call is made by males in isolation. It might be a way for the male to announce his presence in an area, as well as his level of arousal or excitement.

Elimination Behaviors

Chinchillas have some elimination behaviors that may seem very strange to most of us but are perfectly normal for chins. Understanding these behaviors is helpful because they have a lot to do with your pet's health as well as successful housebreaking.

When a chinchilla urinates, it often places its body in such a way that the urine is eliminated away from and outside of its cage. Wait to see how your pet urinates before you select a permanent place for the cage. This prevents accidents and staining on walls. Chinchillas often choose the same corner of their cage as an area

Be Aware!
Chinchilla urine can form calcified scales on cage pans, so be sure to put enough litter in the litter pan and change it frequently to reduce odors!

to urinate in but are not as careful about defecating. Fecal pellets usually drop randomly about the cage whenever nature calls.

If it seems like your pet is constantly dropping pellets wherever it goes, that is because it is! A chinchilla passes more than 200 fecal pellets in a day!

Coprophagy

Coprophagy is the act of eating feces. Chinchilla fecal pellets contain recyclable nutrients and B vitamins. When a chinchilla performs coprophagy, it bends forward from a sitting position to take the fecal pellet into its mouth as it is passed. This is perfectly normal behavior. In fact, if chinchillas are prevented from eating their droppings, they will suffer health problems.

Housebreaking

Some chins learn to use a litter box for their toilet, just like a cat or a ferret. Teaching your pet to use a litter box is not difficult, but it does require a lot of time, effort, and patience. Not all chins are clever enough to be housebroken!

It is easiest to start with a young chinchilla. Find a leak-proof pan that is easy to clean. Ideally the litter pan should be made of metal. If you use a plastic pan, remember your pet will chew on it. Do not use cardboard. Chinchilla urine is very concentrated, and cardboard will leak and disintegrate!

Cover the floor of the litter pan with shredded paper or paper pellet litter (avoid scented, clay, or clumping litter). Cover the litter with a little bit of straw. This will keep your pet from getting dirty from the litter underneath as it becomes moistened, soiled, and crumbles. It will also make the litter pan seem more attractive to your chinchilla, so your chin will be more likely to go into it and explore.

Collect some of your pet's recent fecal pellets and scatter them in the pan. This is how you show your chin where it should eliminate. By finding fecal pellets already in place, your chinchilla may catch on to the idea faster.

You can also place a flat rock in the litter pan. Many chinchillas prefer to urinate on rocks, just as chinchillas in the wild often do.

Chinchillas are usually selective about where they eliminate. This sounds silly, after discussing how they eliminate in food dishes and dust baths. The fact is, though, most chins keep their nest box and sleeping areas clean. For the most part, chinchillas prefer to urinate in a selected area of the cage.

Take advantage of your pet's habits. Place the litter pan in the corner of the cage where elimination usually takes place. It may take several days, maybe weeks, before your chinchilla gets the idea. If you happen to be there to see your pet eliminate in the litter pan, reward it immediately with a small treat. If all goes well, it will eventually make an association between eliminating in the litter pan and receiving a food reward. Once your chinchilla has started to use the litter pan regularly, you can relocate the pan when your chin goes outside of the cage to play.

Do not be discouraged if your chin does not use a litter pan reliably or never learns to use one at all. Some animals just do not get it. No matter what, never scold your pet, and never hit it. Chinchillas cannot be disciplined. Such cruel actions would only confuse your pet and make it fearful of you. Your chinchilla would never make the association between your displeasure, disciplinary action, and its normal bodily functions. After all, a chinchilla naturally eliminates anytime it feels like it. If you can train your little friend to use a litter pan, even part of the time, that is quite an accomplishment!

Chapter Eight

Chinchilla Health Care

Good news! Keeping your chinchilla healthy is easy! Just follow the "Essentials of Chinchilla Care" and the guidelines on feeding, housing, and basic care provided in this handbook.

Prevention

The most important health care you can give your chinchilla is preventive health care. Preventing health problems is easier than treating them. By giving your precious pet excellent care, you might double its life span from the average of 10 years to a maximum of 20 years or more!

Essentials of Chinchilla Care

- Good, nutritious food
- Fresh water at all times
- A large, roomy, clean cage
- An exercise wheel
- Dust baths
- Lots of space to run and play
- Clean, dry, draft-free housing
- Comfortable temperature and humidity (avoid hot places!)
- Quiet, interesting environment
- Hideaways and nest boxes
- Chew toys to keep teeth healthy
- Interesting, safe toys

- A home that avoids exposure to other animals, especially other rodents
- Lots of love and attention from you

If Your Chinchilla Is Sick

Sometimes even animals that receive the very best care can become ill. Without the right kind of care, a sick chinchilla can quickly weaken and die. Chinchillas try to hide their illnesses so they will not appear vulnerable to predators. This means that it is not always easy to know when your pet is sick unless you know your pet very well and are observing it closely. By the time you realize your companion is sick, it could be much sicker than you think. If the illness is advanced, it will be very difficult for your pet to recover.

If your chinchilla shows any signs that it does not feel well, contact your veterinarian immediately. *The sooner your chinchilla's health problem is diagnosed and treated, the better your pet's chances are for recovery.*

Ways to Tell If Your Chinchilla Is Healthy

	Healthy	*Sick*
Appearance	Bright, clear eyes; beautiful, soft, plush coat; robust, compact body; normal weight for size	Dull expression, squinty eyes, discharge from eyes, coat in poor condition, patches of hair loss, wet chin, weight loss, thin, diarrhea, or constipation
Behavior	Alert, good appetite, drinking, vocalizing, social, playful, inquisitive, interested in surroundings, normal urination and defecation	Lethargic, depressed, not eating or drinking, quiet (little or no vocalization), abnormal elimination (diarrhea, constipation, or "chain stools"), retching, drooling, abnormal body position when sitting or lying down, excessive rolling (pain)

Signs of Illness

You can be sure something is wrong if your chinchilla:

- Has abnormal or unusual fecal pellets, diarrhea, or constipation
- Acts lethargic (sluggish)
- Has a dull, poor-quality, or patchy coat
- Is hunched up or lying down in an abnormal position
- Is not eating or drinking
- Is drooling
- Has trouble breathing
- Has a foul odor (from its mouth, skin, or anus)
- Does not want to use the dust bath
- Does not want to play
- Is not interested in you or its surroundings

Be sure to seek supportive care and advice from your veterinarian if

Important signs of a sick chinchilla include abnormal feces, lethargy, lack of appetite, dehydration, hunched-up position, poor coat condition, breathing difficulties, foul odors, and drooling.

The Typical Chinchilla

Life span	10 to 20 years
Body temperature (rectal)	96 to 102.2°F (35.8 to 39°C), females tend to have higher rectal temperatures than males.
Heart rate	100 to 150 beats per minute
Respiratory rate	40 to 80 breaths per minute
Weight	Males: (slightly smaller than females) 0.88 to 1.3 pounds (400 to 600 g) Females: 0.88 to 1.77 pounds (400 to 800 g)

your chinchilla exhibits any signs of illness.

Do Not Take Chances

Chinchilla health problems can be challenging to diagnose. This is because many of the signs and symptoms of chinchilla illness are the same, but the causes may be different. For example, diarrhea is easy to recognize, yet it can look the same whether it is due to the wrong kinds of food, intestinal parasites, infection, or stress. You can treat the *symptoms*, but the *cause* of the problem needs to be identified in order to find a cure. Your veterinarian plays a key role in helping you make an accurate diagnosis.

Do not take chances with your chinchilla's health. You can find lots of home remedies for chinchilla ailments in pet books, magazines, and through the Internet, but be very careful! Some of the remedies are effective, some are not. Some are safe, some are not. Some "remedies" may even make the problem worse or kill your pet. *Before you give your chinchilla any kind of medication or treatment, always ask your veterinarian for advice.*

We have more information available today about chinchillas than we have ever had. With so many people keeping chinchillas as pets, interest and knowledge continues to grow. Fur farmers of decades past have left us a lot of information about raising chinchillas in large colonies. Some of the health problems encountered in large colonies, and the kinds of treatments the animals received, were based on colony or herd medicine. Fur farmers had to treat hundreds, sometimes thousands, of permanently caged animals with no hope of longevity because they were destined to become pelts.

Fortunately, pet chinchillas are raised under different conditions and for a different purpose. So it makes sense that the right treatment for a pet chinchilla might not be the same treatment given to large chinchilla colonies 50 years ago. Even if your

If your chinchilla is acting lethargic or depressed, handle it gently and contact your veterinarian immediately.

How You Can Help

You can do a lot to help your pet when it is sick, while awaiting guidance from your veterinarian. So look at some safe ways you can start your pet on the road to recovery.

1. The moment you notice your chinchilla is ill, separate it from your other chinchillas. This way, if the problem is contagious, you have reduced the chances of spreading the disease to your other pets. Isolating your sick chinchilla gives it a chance to begin its recuperation in peace and quiet without distraction and stress. Place your chinchilla in a comfortable, dark, quiet place. Rest is an important key to recovery.

2. Next, contact your veterinarian for advice. An accurate diagnosis is important. It is the only way to know what the problem is, if it is contagious to you or your other pets, and if prescription medication can help. Sometimes prescription medication is necessary to ensure your chinchilla's survival, but sometimes all your pet needs is good supportive, tender loving home care.

3. Handling and transportation can seriously upset a sick chinchilla, so try to transport your pet as gently as possible. Reduce stress by allowing it to travel in a hideaway house or tunnel placed in a small travel kennel. Loud and unusual sounds frighten chinchillas, so cover the travel kennel with a large, dark towel to reduce noises and light that can startle and stress your small companion.

pet suffers from one of the same health problems as its less-fortunate, commercially raised ancestors, its future is much brighter because it can benefit from good veterinary care, modern medicine, and individualized attention. Your chinchilla deserves the best care you can give it, so do not risk your pet's health by using old remedies. Always ask your veterinarian which treatment is the safest and best for your pet.

Do not waste precious time experimenting with home remedies when you are not sure of the safety of the remedy or the cause of the health problem. Do not hesitate to talk to your veterinarian whenever you have a question or concern.

4. Continue to keep a close watch on your other chinchillas, and separate out any others that may begin to shows signs of illness.

5. Thoroughly wash all housing, toys, dishes, and bottles that were in contact with your sick pet.

6. Discard all food and bedding that were in contact with your sick chinchilla, and clean and disinfect the cage. Be sure to check the food and hay for signs of mold and bad odors.

7. Check the label on your pet's food to see if there have been changes in ingredients made by the manufacturer and to be sure the food is not outdated.

8. Wash your hands thoroughly after handling your sick pet and before handling other pets or food. Wear disposable gloves, and change your clothes in between handling sick and well animals. Always handle sick animals *after* handling the well ones. All of these precautions will help prevent possible spread of contagious disease.

Helping Your Veterinarian

Make a list of all the questions you want to ask your veterinarian. In your hurry and concern, you might forget to ask something important later on. If you have made a note of it now, you will be prepared.

Your veterinarian will ask you questions and rely on your answers to help make a diagnosis and deter-

If your pet is sick, do not waste time or endanger its life with home remedies. Contact your veterinarian for advice.

Caution!
Never give your chinchilla any medication that was not specifically prescribed for it! Your veterinarian's expertise in this regard is absolutely necessary!

mine what kind of treatment is necessary. You will be speaking for your pet. The better you know your chinchilla and the more information you have, the better spokesperson you will be. Do not worry if you do not have all the answers. No one ever does. However, every piece of information you have will help your pet.

Before your veterinary appointment, make a list of the following information:

• Age of your chinchilla
• Where your pet was obtained, and how long you have owned it

Bright eyes, an alert expression, a beautiful coat, and normal fecal pellets are all signs of a healthy chinchilla.

- When you first noticed the problem
- Any signs of discomfort, pain, or difficulty breathing
- What you have done, if anything, so far to treat the problem
- Last time your chinchilla ate or drank
- Last time your chinchilla urinated or defecated
- Size, form, color, and consistency of stools (with particular attention to diarrhea, constipation, or blood in the feces)
- Signs of drooling or inability to chew
- Number and type of other pets at home
- Number of animals housed in the same cage with your sick chinchilla (remember to mention any animals that you have recently acquired)

- Type and amount of food you give your chinchilla, including special treats or any recent change in diet
- Housing and environmental conditions (temperature and humidity), any recent changes in conditions, and cage-cleaning schedule
- Possible exposure to sick animals, poisonous plants, toxins, drafts, heat
- If your chinchilla is pregnant, give information about any previous pregnancies or problems
- Mention anything else you can think of that might help in determining the cause of illness and how to treat it.

Health Problems

More than 40 years ago, chinchilla breeders reported that half of the deaths on their chinchilla fur farms were caused by digestive tract problems. Of these deaths, 25 percent were due to dental malocclusion (misalignment of the teeth). Today, the most common causes of illness in pet chinchillas are still related to digestive tract disorders. These are due to errors in feeding (diet, nutrition) and husbandry (cage size, bedding, and sanitation). In other words, the wrong kind of diet and poor husbandry remain the key culprits in chinchilla diseases and ailments. The good news is that you have full control over your pet's diet and husbandry. So when you know what is best for your chinchilla, keeping it healthy is easy!

Detecting early illness in chinchillas can be challenging because pet chinchillas still maintain behaviors typical of their wild ancestors. For example, chinchillas are stoic and try to hide their illnesses the best they can as a survival mechanism. By acting like they are well, even though they are sick, chinchillas will not appear weak and vulnerable to predators. Unfortunately, this means that by the time you notice your pet is sick, it is probably *very* sick and its illness may have progressed to a late stage, making it more difficult to treat successfully.

The following section about possible health problems may seem very long. Don't let this list frighten or discourage you. Chinchillas are healthy, happy animals when they receive good care and nutrition. However, when a chinchilla is sick, it becomes very fragile and its health can rapidly deteriorate in a very short time. Use this information to your advantage so you can recognize health problems in your chinchilla when they first occur and provide immediate first aid.

Digestive Tract Problems

Because the most common chinchilla illnesses today are due to problems with the digestive tract, we will talk about these first and in detail. The chinchilla's digestive tract is very long, about 120 inches (300 cm) or longer. It extends from the mouth to the esophagus (the tube leading from the mouth to the stomach), to the stomach, through the intestines and cecum, to the colon (large intestine), and then to the rectum.

Did You Know?

Chinchillas, rats, and horses share some common anatomical and physiological features, including:
1. They do not have a gallbladder.
2. They cannot vomit.

Digestive tract disorders may be contagious (spreading from one animal to the other through infection or parasites) or noncontagious. Fortunately, most digestive tract problems in chinchillas are noncontagious. Problems such as malocclusion or eating the wrong foods are examples of problems that cause noncontagious digestive tract problems. Conditions caused by bacteria (such as *Clostridium*, *Escherichia*, *Proteus*, and *Salmonella*) or parasites (such as protozoa and worms) are contagious, or infectious. Whatever the cause of your pet's digestive tract upset, the symptoms may be the same, although the proper treatment for each condition may be different. So take a closer look at how to recognize different causes of digestive tract disorders, how to treat them, and most important of all—how to prevent them.

Bloat (gastric tympany) is the accumulation of gas within the gastrointestinal tract. Gas and fluid can accumulate anywhere along the intestines and inside the stomach, causing the abdomen to swell and distend. It is astounding how large and round your pet can look and how grossly enlarged and tight its belly can feel. A chinchilla with bloat is in great pain and tries to relieve the

Serious Scatology*

Most illnesses in chinchillas are related to gastrointestinal tract problems. The best way to recognize (and stop!) gastrointestinal problems early on is by closely examining your pet's fecal pellets (also known as droppings, bowel movements, excrements, feces, scats, and stools).

Paying attention to your pet's eliminations is one of the most important things you can do to know if it is healthy. It's also one of the easiest things to do!

Fecal Facts:

• Healthy chinchillas pass more than 200 fecal pellets daily!
• Chinchillas defecate between 3:00 A.M. and 6:00 A.M.
• Chinchillas consume cecotropes between 8:00 A.M. and 2:00 P.M.

Perfect Pellets:

• Normal fecal pellets from healthy chinchillas are brown, dark gray, or black and are dry and about ½ inch (approximately 1 cm) in length.
• Fecal size varies with the size of the animal.
• Fecal pellets from males are usually longer and narrower.
• Morning fecal pellets are smaller than evening fecal pellets.
• Normal pellets are plump, odorless, and oblong shaped (like large grains of rice). Any other type of pellet means your pet needs immediate care.

Problem Pellets:

• Fecal pellets that contain blood; have a foul odor; are soft or mushy, shiny, moist and bubbly, or "chained" together with bits of hair are signs of a problem.

*Scatology: the study of feces

pain by lying down, stretching on its side, and rolling. After a while, the animal is reluctant to move, and as gas continues to accumulate, pressure builds up against the diaphragm and lungs, and breathing becomes difficult. Sometimes there are no gut sounds, and sometimes it is possible to hear gas gurgling in the abdomen. Fecal pellets may have tiny gas and mucous bubbles on them.

Causes of bloat include overeating, a rapid change in diet, the wrong foods, too many fresh greens and fruits, gas-producing foods, infections, and obstructions of the gastrointestinal tract. If your chinchilla is raising a litter of kits, pay close attention to her. Bloat is not uncommon in lactating (milk-producing) females two to three weeks after they give birth. (Sometimes paralysis of the hind limbs also occurs in postpartum females, possibly caused by a drop in calcium blood levels due to milk production.)

Bloat is a life-threatening emergency. It is extremely painful and can quickly lead to death. Do not wait. Contact your veterinarian immediately. The stomach needs to be decompressed, and your pet may also need calcium (in the form of injectable calcium gluconate).

You can help prevent bloat by feeding your chinchilla a healthy, balanced diet and by not feeding it too many greens and fruits. Including a mineral block in the cage that contains calcium can also be beneficial.

Choke: Chinchillas cannot vomit or regurgitate. If your pet aspirates

Digestive tract problems are the most common cause of chinchilla illness and death. You can prevent these problems by feeding your pet a healthy diet made specifically for chinchillas and by providing fresh hay daily.

food into its trachea (windpipe, the tube leading to the lungs), it can suffer from choke and quickly die of asphyxiation (suffocation). Drooling, retching, breathing difficulty, and refusal to eat are all signs of choke.

Chinchillas of all ages can suffer from choke, especially animals that eat small treats (raisins, bits of fruit, nuts) or foreign objects (such as bedding material). Female chinchillas that have just given birth may suffer from choke after eating the placentas (afterbirth) of their kits. Eating placentas is not unusual behavior for female chinchillas.

If your chinchilla is choking, the foreign object or food has to be removed. Surgery might be necessary. Time is critical, so do not waste a second. If you can see the object and you can grab hold of it safely with tweezers or small forceps (be careful not to get bitten!), you might

be able to pull the obstruction out. However, this is difficult and unlikely because the chinchilla's mouth and throat are small and narrow. The important thing is not to push the object accidentally down the throat and make the problem worse.

You can help prevent choke by feeding your pet the right foods, avoiding excess treats, and keeping the cage free of foreign objects that can be easily chewed into tiny pieces (for example, bits of rubber, string, plastic).

Caution!
Do not give your chinchilla kaopectate or Pepto-Bismol or similar products. The formula for these medications has recently changed to include a substance that is toxic to some species of animals (including cats), and the new formula has not been proven safe for chinchillas.

Constipation occurs more often than diarrhea in chinchillas, yet it often goes unnoticed. If your chinchilla is straining to defecate or is passing less fecal pellets than usual, and if the pellets are hard, dry, thin, short, or have blood on them, then your chinchilla is constipated. Constipation and straining to defecate can cause rectal prolapse, a serious condition that can include partial prolapse of the colon. When not successfully treated, it can lead to death.

Constipation is easy to prevent because it is usually caused by not feeding enough roughage (fiber). Insufficient fluid intake can also add to the problem. Your pet's digestive system evolved to accommodate a high-fiber diet rich in roughage. Chinchillas in the wild prefer plants that contain the most fiber. Like its wild ancestors, your chinchilla needs lots of fresh grass hay to munch at all times. It also needs to have fresh water available at all times.

Pregnant chinchillas can suffer from constipation as the fetuses developing in the uterus (in utero) become so large they press against her intestines. Once the kits are born, the problem usually goes away.

Overweight or inactive chinchillas can also be constipated. Treatment for them is a gradual, safe, weight reduction program accomplished by eliminating excess snacks and treats, increasing fiber in the diet, and giving the animal more opportunities to play and exercise. If your pet does not already have an exercise wheel (it should!), now is the time to buy it one!

If you see that your pet is constipated, give it more roughage and increase fiber in the diet by adding small pieces of fresh apple. Do not feed nuts, raisins, or any grains. Add a little bit of vegetable oil to the diet. A veterinary laxative product (Laxatone) or product to remove hair balls (Petramalt) may be helpful in making the fecal pellets slick and easier to move out. In more serious cases of constipation, your veterinarian can show you how to properly give a gentle enema. *Do not use Fleet enemas; some types are toxic to animals.*

You can help prevent constipation by giving your pet sufficient roughage in its daily feeding to stimulate intestinal transit and keep intestinal contents moving. Make sure fresh water is available at all times.

Diarrhea is loose, watery stools. If the condition is serious, it can quickly lead to dehydration and death. Because chinchillas groom themselves and clean their fur frequently, it is possible to overlook diarrhea. If your chinchilla is depressed, lethargic, dehydrated, or has a dull, poor-quality coat, it may have diarrhea. Check for staining and dampness around the anus. Check the wire mesh, floor pans, and resting boards for signs of loose or smeared feces, indicative of diarrhea.

Acute or sudden-onset diarrhea is often caused by feeding too many fresh greens, moldy hay, or young hay (hay more than six months old is recommended). It can also be caused by protozoal infections (*Giardia, Cryptosporidium*). Acute diarrhea is serious, life threatening, and needs immediate medical treatment.

Chronic or gradual-onset and prolonged diarrhea can be due to bacterial or parasitic infections. Severe diarrhea can lead to rectal prolapse.

Until the cause of diarrhea can be found and corrected, make sure your pet does not become dehydrated or suffer from an electrolye imbalance. Diarrhea causes rapid dehydration, and dehydration can quickly lead to death. If necessary, add electrolytes to your chinchilla's drinking water. A small, plain (not sugared or salted!) shredded wheat biscuit might help slow the diarrhea if your pet will eat it. However, you must contact your veterinarian immediately for help and to check your pet's electrolyte balance.

If your pet refuses to eat or drink and you cannot give it fluids by mouth, it may need fluids given under

Long Intestines!
The total length of an adult chinchilla's intestinal tract can be more than 135 inches long (approximately 350 cm)!

the skin (subcutaneously). Your veterinarian will do this or may show you how to do it. If the diarrhea is caused by bacteria or parasites, a prescription medication may be necessary.

A gastric trichobezoar "hair ball" is as strange as it sounds. It is a foreign object in the stomach or intestinal tract—a concretion made of hair. A trichobezoar can be described as a firm hair ball. Chinchillas may swallow some hair when they groom themselves, but chinchillas that are fur chewers swallow a lot of hair.

Lack of appetite, depression, lethargy, and abdominal pain are all warning signs of hair balls. Some chinchilla (and rabbit) breeders feed fresh pineapple juice or papaya tablets to treat hair balls because they believe the enzymes in pineapples and papaya break down fur balls in an animal's stomach. Veterinary products such as Laxatone and Petramalt might help eliminate hair balls, unfortunately trichobezoars usually need to be surgically removed.

The best way to prevent hair balls is to separate animals that chew on one another and make sure all animals receive a good diet. Research has suggested that fur chewing may be due to a nutritional imbalance or

Most Common Noncontagious Disorders of the Digestive Tract

Problem	Symptoms	Cause
Gastric tympany, bloat	Enlarged, swollen abdomen; reluctance to move; difficulty breathing; animal lies on its sides	Change in diet, excess fresh greens and fruits, overeating; seen most often in lactating females two to three weeks after giving birth
Choke	Drooling, retching, lack of appetite, difficulty breathing, suffocating, foreign object may be aspirated from esophagus into trachea "windpipe"	Chinchillas cannot vomit and are unable to regurgitate small particles that may choke them; occurs in chinchillas of any age, more often in those that eat small treats—raisins, fruits, nuts—or eat foreign objects, such as bedding material
Slobbers	Drooling; mouth may have foul odor; wet chin, chest, and forepaws; weight loss; gradual wasting; and finally death from starvation	Inability to swallow or pain, often associated with malocclusion of the cheek teeth
Constipation	Straining and difficulty defecating; hard, thin, short fecal pellets; may have blood on feces; may need radiographs (X rays) to identify exact cause and location, especially in cases of impaction or foreign body obstruction	Feeding too much concentrated diet without feeding enough fiber or roughage; obesity, insufficient exercise, or lack of activity; pregnant females may have constipation caused by fetal pressure on intestines
Diarrhea	Watery feces smeared in cage, fur around anus matted with feces or stained	Sudden onset, often caused by incorrect diet, such as overfeeding green foods or feeding moldy hay; gradual onset, often caused by bacterial and parasitic infections

malnutrition. Some chinchilla breeders think the problem is a hereditary behavioral disorder. Fur chewing might also be caused by boredom, in which case providing your pet with lots of interesting toys and space to play can certainly help relieve boredom and might help prevent fur-chewing. Finally, adding a product such as Petramalt to your pet's diet is another easy preventive measure you can take.

Treatment	Prevention
Emergency situation that requires decompression of the stomach and possibly calcium injection(s) to prevent rapid, painful death	Correct diet, good husbandry, do not feed fresh greens and fruit in excess, closely monitor lactating females
Immediate veterinary care, sedation, tracheostomy (make an open airway for breathing) and removal of foreign object	Correct diet and good husbandry
Trim and file affected teeth	Eliminate affected animals from the breeding program
Increase fiber in the diet by adding small amounts of fresh apples; eliminate raisins, grains, and other treats; laxatives if necessary (consult your veterinarian for type and dose)	Add a small amount of vegetable oil to feed, provide sufficient amount of fiber in diet
Correct diet, add electrolyes to drinking water, make sure animal remains well hydrated, and give subcutaneous fluids if necessary	Good diet, parasite control

Stomach (gastric) ulcers: When chinchillas are fed bad hay, moldy hay, or hay that is too rough and coarse, they can develop stomach ulcers. Young chinchillas are most susceptible to developing ulcers. Often the only symptoms are lack of appetite and overall poor condition. Sometimes the ulcer is not discovered until necropsy (animal autopsy). Ulcers can often be diagnosed by radiography (X ray). Your veterinarian

Most Common Noncontagious Disorders of the Digestive Tract (continued)

Problem	Symptoms	Cause
Gastroenteritis	Diarrhea, dehydration, weight loss, painful abdomen	Change in diet, contaminated feed, misuse of certain antibiotics
Gastric torsion (twisting), intussusception (inward tele-scoping of the intestines), and fecal impaction of the colon	Hunched-up position, lying down stretched out, or rolling, all in an effort to relieve the intense pain caused by these conditions.	Chronic constipation or gastroenteritis
Gastric ulcers (stomach ulcers)	Lack of appetite, often stomach ulcers are not discovered until after death	Seen more often in young chinchillas, lack of appetite and attempts to regurgitate
Rectal prolapse	Enlarged, swollen, painful, reddened, protruding anus (rectum and in some cases intestines)	Chronic constipation, straining, chronic diarrhea
Trichobezoar "hair ball"	Unusual body position, depressed, lethargic, lack of appetite, abdominal pain	Eating fur, fur chewing

can prescribe medication to coat and protect the lining of your pet's stomach while it heals.

Gastroenteritis is inflammation of the stomach and intestines. It is often caused by a change in diet or by feeding contaminated food.

Diarrhea, dehydration, weight loss, abdominal pain, unusual posture (hunched up sitting or stretched out lying down to relieve the pain),

and rectal prolapse are all signs of gastroenteritis. Your chin can have one or several of these symptoms.

Treat gastroenteritis by giving your pet enough roughage in the diet. Stop feeding any food that might be contaminated and give supportive care (fluids, electrolytes, quiet stress-free environment). *Lactobacillus acidophilus* will help reestablish your pet's normal intestinal flora. (*Lacto-*

Treatment	Prevention
Roughage, (sometimes a small amount of dry, shredded wheat may help control diarrhea), supportive care, *Lactobacillus acidophilus*	Good diet, fresh food
Gastric torsion and intussusception are life threatening and surgery is necessary, impaction may be treated with warm, gentle mineral oil enemas	Good nutrition and prevention of constipation and gastroenteritis
Avoid coarse, rough food and contact your veterinarian for medication to coat and protect the lining of the stomach	Do not feed coarse, rough, or moldy hay or food
May sometimes be reduced by coating rectum with mineral oil and gently pressing rectum back into place; often surgery (stay sutures) are required; follow with bland cereal diet while healing	Good diet, prevention of constipation and diarrhea
Surgery may be necessary	Prevent fur chewing, feed a nutritious diet, offer lots of toys and play time to prevent boredom

bacillus acidophilus is a species of "good bacteria" for the intestines and is available from your veterinarian or health food store either in a gel, paste, or liquid or in yogurt cultures.)

Intestinal torsion and impaction: Chronic gastroenteritis or constipation can lead to intestinal torsion (twisting of the intestines) and impaction of the cecum and colon. Intussusception (the intestines tele-scope or fold inside themselves) can also occur. All of these conditions are extremely painful. Death may follow in a very short time.

Chinchillas suffering from intestinal torsion or impaction hunch up or lie down and stretch out. They will roll in an effort to relieve the intense pain.

This extremely painful condition is a life-threatening emergency that

Chinchillas love company. If your pet isolates itself from you or its companions, or if it acts withdrawn or unfriendly, it probably is not feeling well.

needs immediate surgery. Unfortunately, even with surgery, chances of survival are not good.

Rectal prolapse: In cases of severe diarrhea or constipation, the rectum can prolapse (protrude), redden, and swell so that it is difficult to return it to its normal position. If the condition is very serious, part of the colon can also protrude and swell,

---

If Your Chinchilla Stops Eating

If your chinchilla stops eating, something is seriously wrong. Take immediate action! When a chinchilla stops eating, it quickly weakens and can die in a short time. Do not lose a moment. Contact your veterinarian immediately for a diagnosis and treatment.

---

and if not treated, the tissues can die (necrose). Rectal prolapse is not unusual in chinchillas. In one report, rectal prolapse was responsible for 6 percent of laboratory chinchilla deaths.

If the rectum is not seriously damaged, it may be possible to coat the exposed portion with a sterile lubricant and a concentrated sugar solution (to help shrink down the tissues) and gently press it back into place. Unfortunately, in many cases, the rectum tends to prolapse again and may need to be corrected surgically and held in place with sutures until the swelling goes down and the tissues heal. During this time, a bland, soft diet of cereals (no rice) is fed for one to two weeks.

Emergency High-Energy Feeding Formula

A commercial critical care diet, such as the one available from Oxbow Pet Products (or from your veterinarian), should be kept on hand at all times. Although many authors have offered various "emergency" feeding formulas, most of these are not properly balanced and may cause dehydration or harmful hyperglycemia (blood sugar levels elevated above normal levels).

A sick chinchilla is a very fragile animal. Rather than risk worsening your little friend's condition, consult your veterinarian and keep a critical care diet on hand at all times. You will have to discard the diet and replace it every three months to be sure it is fresh and keeps the nutritional value that is so important for your chinchilla's recovery, but that is a small price to pay to protect your pet's health in case of emergency.

If you are unable to give your chinchilla food or liquids with a syringe, contact your veterinarian immediately. In most cases, aggressive medical therapy is necessary, including fluid therapy and, in very serious cases, passing a feeding tube directly into the stomach to prevent starvation and death.

Bacteria, Parasites, and Protozoa

Bacteria (germs), intestinal parasites (such as worms), and protozoa (amoeba-like microscopic organisms) can cause such serious gastroenteritis that a chinchilla can die suddenly without warning signs. Fortunately, most problems are less sudden and severe. If you see the

If your pet's coat loses its plush quality and luster and is matted, greasy, or patchy, consult your veterinarian. A poor coat is often a sign of an underlying health problem.

warning signs, usually in the form of chronic diarrhea, then you have time to take immediate action.

Bacterial gastroenteritis: Chinchillas have a special kind of diges-

---

Lactobacillus acidophilus, "Good" Bacteria

Too many of the wrong bacteria, known as Gram-negative bacteria, can cause diarrhea and sudden death in your pet. These bacteria include *Escherichia coli (E. coli), Proteus, Salmonella,* and *Clostridium.* If your chinchilla has diarrhea, feed it the Gram-positive bacteria *Lactobacillus acidophilus.* If your chinchilla is on antibiotics, *Lactobacillus acidophilus* can help reduce diarrhea or bacterial flora imbalance caused by antibiotic therapy. *Lactobacillus acidophilus* is available from your health food store in liquid or yogurt culture or in gel or paste form from your veterinarian.

Most Common Contagious (Infectious) Disorders of the Digestive Tract

Problem	Symptoms	Cause
Bacterial gastroenteritis	Diarrhea, abdominal pain, lack of appetite, poor condition, weight loss, lethargy, death; Corynebacterial enteritis also causes peritonitis, abscesses in the gut, and hind limb paralysis	Gram-negative bacteria: *Escherichia, Proteus, Salmonella, Clostridium, Corynebacteria*
Protozoal enteritis	Some chinchillas may not show signs of infection, others may show signs such as weight loss, wasting, diarrhea, and bloody feces	*Giardia, Trichomonas, Balantidium, Cryptosporidium, Eimeria*
Parasitic enteritis	Some chinchillas may not show signs of disease unless they are heavily infested, others may suffer from inflammation of the colon and diarrhea	Worms: trematodes, nematodes, cestodes, *Physaloptera, Hymenolepis, Haemonchus*

tive system that depends on "good bacteria" living in their intestinal tracts. These bacteria are necessary for your pet's health and normal digestion. The bacteria are called Gram-positive bacteria (this name comes from how they look under the microscope when using a special stain, Gram's stain, to view them). "Good" Gram-positive bacteria that live in a healthy chinchilla's intestine are *Bifidobacterium*, *Bacteriodes*, *Eubacterium*, and *Lactobacillus*. Their names are long and intimidating, but they are the intestinal flora that are important for your pet's health.

Signs of bacterial, protozoal, and parasitic gastroenteritis include diarrhea, lack of appetite, abdominal pain, and lethargy. Bacterial gastroenteritis is usually caused by feeding contaminated food and the wrong types of food. It can also be caused by giving the wrong kinds of antibiotics, leading to an overgrowth of harmful bacteria. In fact, some antibiotics used to treat disease kill the "good" bacteria along with the "bad" bacteria. For example, antibiotics such as erythromycin, clindamycin, and lincomycin will kill the "good" Gram-positive bacteria your pet so desperately needs for normal digestion. So be careful!

Do not give your chinchilla any medicine that has been prescribed for you or one of your other pets.

Do not give your chinchilla any medicine that has not been specifically prescribed for it and for its current medical condition.

Note: Albendazole is the drug of choice for treatment of *Giardia*. It is safe and more efficacious than

Treatment	Prevention
Feed correct diet and give *Lactobacillus acidophilus* to help restore Gram-positive bacteria in the intestinal tract; antibiotics (the correct kind!) may be necessary, so consult your veterinarian	Avoid feeding contaminated food, keep pet isolated from affected animals
Antiprotozoal medication is available from your veterinarian; keep your pet hydrated, and give it electrolytes	Fresh, clean water; good food; good husbandry (keep housing environment dry); reduce stress; isolate and treat affected animals
Anthelmintic (worm-killing medication) available from your veterinarian	Good hygiene, good husbandry, clean housing, clean water, avoid feeding contaminated food, isolate and treat affected animals

metronidazole. Metronidazole is not recommended for young animals or those with impaired liver function.

Dental Problems

Chinchilla teeth (incisors and molars) are open rooted and grow throughout life. The outer surface of the incisors is covered with enamel and is harder than the inside material and back of the tooth, which consists of dentin. So as your chinchilla chews, its teeth are constantly chiseled and sharpened. There are no nerves in the incisors, except at the base of the tooth where growth takes place.

Check your chinchilla regularly for dental problems. You can do this by using a small cloth sling to lift the upper jaw gently, revealing the front incisors. If you prefer, your veterinar-ian can perform the dental examina-tion for you.

Most dental problems can be avoided by providing safe chew toys and a balanced diet. Some dental problems, such as malocclusion or malformation of the roof of the mouth (palate), are considered by many to be hereditary.

Malocclusion: When the incisors (front teeth) or molars (cheek teeth) do not grow in proper alignment, the teeth wear unevenly. This is called *malocclusion* and is a common prob-lem in chinchillas. Malocclusion can be acquired, congenital, or heredi-tary. An acquired condition is one that develops after birth from some cause, such as trauma or an acci-dent. Congenital means the animal had the condition from birth. A con-genital problem may or may not be

Most Common Dental Problems

Problem	Symptom	Cause
Malocclusion	Misaligned or misdirected, protruding teeth, loss of appetite, weight loss, depression, drooling, wet chin, inability to swallow, painful mouth, "slobbers"	May be inherited or caused by trauma, possibly caused by poor diet
Broken teeth, gum infection, periodontal disease	Reluctance to eat, weight loss, pain, drooling, protruding teeth	Trauma

hereditary. If a condition is hereditary, it is acquired genetically. In other words, the animal has received the gene(s) for the trait from its parent(s)

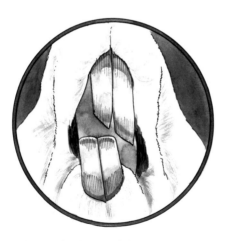

Malocclusion is one of the most common medical problems in chinchillas. The teeth need to be trimmed regularly throughout the animal's life. Because the condition may be inherited, affected animals should not be used for breeding.

and the animal is capable of passing the condition to its own offspring.

Remember that early chinchilla farmers attributed 50 percent of chinchilla deaths to problems of the digestive tract. Of this 50 percent, 25 percent were caused by malocclusion. In other words, more than 10 percent of deaths (12.5 percent to be exact) were considered to be related to malocclusion. That's a significant percentage and a big loss of animals. So if you plan to raise chinchillas, it's very important to cull (remove, eliminate) animals with dental problems from the breeding program.

Malocclusion can be very painful because one or more of the misdirected teeth can grow into the delicate tissues of the mouth. Chinchillas may have malocclusion of the incisors or the molars. Misaligned molars may curve inward and outward from each other. The molars

Treatment	Prevention
Trim and file affected teeth, give pain medication as needed, and in all cases use only medicines prescribed by your veterinarian	Eliminate affected animals from breeding programs, feed a good diet
To prevent injury to the mouth, the tooth opposite the broken tooth needs to be trimmed until the broken tooth grows back; for cases of gum and periodontal disease, vitamin C supplementation may be beneficial; consult your veterinarian for a recommended dose; give pain medication as needed (prescribed by your veterinarian)	Prevent trauma

overgrow laterally, causing trauma to the mouth and injuring the tongue or inside of the cheeks. Malocclusion can also cause abscesses, periodontal disease, and inflammation of the bone surrounding the teeth in the jaw. These painful conditions may exist on one or both sides of the jaw, making it difficult or impossible for the animal to eat.

If your chinchilla is drooling or has a wet chin (from the accumulation of excess saliva), has protruding teeth or trouble swallowing, is losing weight or refusing to eat, or has a painful mouth or a foul odor coming from it, there is a very good chance it is suffering from dental malocclusion.

Detecting the problem simply by looking is not easy because your chinchilla's mouth is small and seeing inside to examine it is difficult. This is a job for your veterinarian. Special skill, special equipment, and anesthesia are required to get a good look deep inside the mouth and to correct the problem. Your chinchilla will suffer and can starve to death if you do not take it to your veterinarian as soon as you notice signs of dental problems. Often it is necessary to trim the offending teeth, file the molars or premolars, or trim the incisors. Sometimes a tooth extraction is required.

After treatment, regular dental maintenance for the life of your pet is the rule.

Trimming a pet's incisors and filing the molars is a job for your veterinarian. Great care must be taken not to fracture the teeth accidentally.

Malocclusion May Be Inherited
Chinchillas that have malocclusion should not be used in a breeding program.

Gas anesthesia is usually required for more extensive dental work. Even though there is no nerve sensation in the upper part of the teeth, extractions can be painful, especially if there are abscesses and bone involvement.

"Slobbers" is just what it sounds like. It is drooling due to excessive salivation, caused by an inability to swallow or pain. "Slobbers" is often associated with malocclusion of the molars, but it can also be caused by infections and abscesses, foreign object obstruction in the mouth, or broken teeth causing sores on the mouth or tongue. "Slobbers" is accompanied by weight loss, gradual wasting, and eventually death from starvation.

Broken teeth: Sometimes an incisor will break. This is usually caused by trauma, such as snagging and breaking a tooth on the wire mesh of a cage. The tooth will grow back. During that time, though, the tooth opposite the missing or broken tooth may become overgrown because it has nothing to mesh and grind against. To prevent injury to the mouth, the opposite tooth needs to be trimmed back until the broken tooth grows back.

Gum infection and tooth loss: Gums may become infected, and a tooth may require removal. Your chinchilla may have a swollen mouth and refuse to eat. Tend to this problem right away so your pet does not go hungry and lose weight. Dental extraction is a job for your veterinarian!

Respiratory Problems

Respiratory disease in chinchillas is usually caused by poor housing conditions. Overcrowding, inadequate ventilation, cold drafts, and high humidity are all factors that can lead to serious problems, such as pneumonia, especially in young or weak chinchillas.

Take a Deep Breath!

Chinchillas have seven lung lobes, three on the left and four on the right. The trachea (windpipe) has an oval shape.

Signs of respiratory problems include difficulty breathing, discharge from the eyes and nose, fever, wheezing, sitting in a hunched position, reluctance to move, and shivering. Pneumonia can be caused by viruses or bacteria. Bacteria that cause respiratory problems in chinchillas include *Streptococcus, Pseudomonas, Pasteurella,* and *Bordetella.*

Treatment should be started right away. Gently clean your pet's eyes and nose, and isolate it from other animals. Place it in a quiet, stress-free, dry, comfortable place. Make sure your chinchilla stays hydrated, and encourage it to eat. Your veterinarian can give you an antibiotic ointment for its eyes and prescribe other medicine as needed. Sadly, if your little friend develops pneumonia, its chances of recovery are not good, even with the help of antibiotics.

Bite Wounds

Chinchillas are choosy about their companions and do not always get along. Females can be aggressive toward males, especially smaller, younger males. Incompatible chinchillas can kill one another. They can become very aggressive during breeding, especially females. So it is not surprising that chinchillas, with their razor-sharp, long teeth, can inflict serious bite wounds. Deep puncture wounds often become infected and form abscesses. Chinchilla conflicts are also responsible for lost pieces of skin, ears, and toes.

If your chinchilla is sick, do your best to encourage it to eat. A vitamin C rich treat might help.

Check your chinchilla for bite wounds by pushing the fur back with your fingers and looking for any lumps, bumps, puncture holes, swelling, redness, tenderness, or pus.

Why Is Cancer Rare in Chinchillas?

Scientists do not yet know why there are so few reports of cancer in chinchillas. Perhaps it is because in the past most chinchillas were used for the fur industry and for laboratory research and did not reach their full age potential. Pet chinchillas are luckier. As we learn more about pet chinchillas, we will no doubt learn the answer to this and many other questions we have about these wonderful animals.

If a bite wound is deep, it can cause serious muscle and nerve damage.

Clean the wound with a mild antiseptic solution, and keep it clean and dry. Let it drain until it has closed on its own and healed. Ask your veterinarian for a topical antibiotic ointment.

You can reduce the incidence of bite wounds by making sure your animals are not overcrowded or overstressed and that they are compatible. *Do not house chinchillas together unless they have been raised together peacefully since birth or you have had enough time to watch them closely and are sure they like each other.*

Dehydration

Dehydration means the animal has lost too much water from its body. One of the most common causes of dehydration in chinchillas is diarrhea. Exposure to a hot, dry environment and illnesses also cause dehydration.

The treatment for dehydration is rehydration, which is replenishing the body with water. If your chinchilla becomes dehydrated, it will lose water and minerals from its body. Give your pet fresh drinking water. Do not try to force water down your chinchilla's throat if it is unconscious or too weak to drink on its own, because it may aspirate the water into its lungs. Give your chinchilla an electrolyte solution (a mixture of water and necessary minerals for rehydration) such as Pedialyte (available over-the-counter from your supermarket or pharmacy). Your veterinarian can also give you an electrolyte solution specially formulated for animals. Always keep a bottle on hand in case of emergency.

Do not give your pet homemade salt or sugar mixtures without consulting your veterinarian. In the wrong proportions, these will do more harm than good and further dehydrate your pet.

Ear Problems

Trauma and infection: Most chinchilla ear problems are caused by trauma (bite wounds on the ear pinnae or hematomas from rubbing the pinnae) or infection. Signs include pain, rubbing the ears, and, in the rare case of inner ear infection, tilting the head to one side (torticollis) and loss of balance.

Treatment is often difficult because the tympanic bulla is fragile. Carefully and gently wipe away any dirt or debris from your pet's ears, and ask your veterinarian for an antibiotic ear ointment. Hematomas require lancing and may need to be sutured.

Yellow ears are generally considered to be caused by a dietary deficiency in choline, methionine, and/or vitamin E. The ears and parts of the body appear yellow because without these substances the liver cannot metabolize plant pigments. In this case, the yellow coloration goes away when the animal is given a good, balanced diet that contains vitamin E, choline, and methionine. However, yellow pigmentation can also be an indication of icterus (jaundice) and liver or other health problems. If your chinchilla has yellow skin pigmentation on *any* part(s) of its body, consult your veterinarian immediately for an accurate diagnosis and correct treatment.

Check your pet's eyes daily. Eye problems are painful and can lead to permanent eye damage. Chinchillas have a vertical slit pupil.

Eye Problems

Chinchillas have big, dark eyes with a vertical slit pupil. Clear, bright, dark eyes add to a chinchilla's beauty. Their eyes are delicate and sensitive. Any eye problem that develops should be taken care of immediately to prevent permanent eye damage or loss of sight.

Eye problems may develop from irritation, injury, or infection. Dust baths can irritate your pet's eyes and cause conjunctivitis (inflammation of the delicate conjunctival tissues surrounding the eyes), especially in young chinchillas.

Vitamin A is important for healthy eyes. Chinchillas that do not receive enough vitamin A in their diet can have frequent tearing, cloudy lenses, and other health problems. Check your pet daily to be sure its eyes are clear and bright. If your chinchilla's eyes are dull, are cloudy, have a dis-

charge (watery or thick), or have stains on the fur around the eyes or if the eyes are squinty or closed, place your pet in a dark room and contact your veterinarian. Many eye problems are painful and make the eyes sensitive to light. Your veterinarian can provide a gentle eyewash and eye ointment or drops. If the problem is caused by a deficiency of vitamin A, your veterinarian will prescribe the correct dose of vitamin A to treat your pet.

Follow veterinary recommendations closely so you do not overdose your pet. Vitamin A excess is as harmful as vitamin A deficiency!

Cataracts and corneal ulcers: Ulcers of the cornea and cataracts both give the eyes a cloudy appearance. However, corneal ulcers are on the surface of the eye and may be caused by injury, such as sharp bed-

Chinchilla Health Problems

Problem	Symptoms	Causes
Bite wounds	Sores, redness, swelling, infection, pain or tenderness, draining pus	Fighting among incompatible animals, female aggression toward a male, overcrowding
Dehydration	When skin is pulled up, it is slow to fall back in place; lethargy, weakness, depression	Diarrhea, heatstroke, infections and diseases, stress
Ear problems	Scratching, discharge from ear, head shaking, loss of balance, head tilted to one side, pain, yellow or red coloration	Trauma, infection
Eye problems	Discharge, watery eyes, cloudy, dull eyes	Infection, injury, irritating substances, disease
Hair loss	Patchy areas of hair loss	*Trichophyton mentagrophytes, Microsporum canis, Microsporum gypseum,* ringworm parasites (mites), fur chewing (barbering), dietary deficiency, stress
Heatstroke	Lying down, rapid breathing, drooling, weak, unresponsive, comatose	High temperatures, high humidity, inadequate ventilation
Infections, septicemias	Symptoms vary and include diarrhea, lethargy, abortions, mastitis, paralysis, loss of balance, head tilt, convulsions, death	Bacteria: *Escherichia coli, Salmonella, Corynebacterium, Pseudomonas, Listeria, Yersinia, Toxoplasmosis*
Respiratory problems	Difficulty breathing, fever, loss of appetite, inactivity, weight loss	Bacteria: *Streptococcus, Pseudomonas, Pasteurella, Bordetella;* also exposure to irritants, fine dusts, drafts, or cold, damp environment

What to Do*

Clean wounds and allow to drain, separate animals that are not compatible

Give fluids, determine and treat cause of problem

Identify and treat cause; if problem is nutritional, correct dietary deficiency

Gently clean eyes with mild eyewash, place in dark area, isolate from other animals, apply prescribed eye ointment

If fungal, treat ringworm; if due to barbering, remove from aggressive, dominant animals; if due to fur chewing, offer more hiding places, toys, space, and attention and make sure the animal is receiving a quality, balanced diet; if due to fur slip, reduce stress and do not handle coat; if dietary, correct deficiency, feed balanced diet; if due to mites, treat

Remove from hot area, submerge body (not head) in tepid water, give fluids as soon as conscious, follow-up veterinary care required

Antibiotics as prescribed, fluids, good nutrition, supportive care

Isolate from other pets, reduce stress, keep comfortable, clean, and dry

ding material or a protruding piece of cage wire mesh scratching or puncturing the surface of the eye. Corneal ulcers are very painful and need to be treated right away to prevent loss of vision and, in some cases, loss of the eye. Cataracts are formed on the lens, inside the eye, and are sometimes seen in older chinchillas.

Important! Use only eye medications that are specifically prescribed for your pet and its current eye problem.

Skin and Hair Problems

Your pet's gorgeous coat is one of the things you love most about it. It is one of the things that makes your pet special and sets it apart from all other animals. No creature can claim a coat as beautiful and as soft as a chinchilla's! So naturally anything that has to do with the health of your little friend's skin and soft, plush fur is very important!

Ringworm is not a worm, it is a skin fungus (dermatophyte). It causes areas of hair loss on the body, especially the nose, behind the ears, and the feet. It starts out small and scaly and makes the coat look patchy. It can progress to large, scabby sores. It is most often caused by *Trichophyton mentagrophytes*, a dermatophyte that is also contagious to humans.

The best treatment for your pet can be determined after your veterinarian makes the diagnosis. Past remedies have included Captan and Griseofulvin. However, they may not be effective in treating the problem,

Chinchilla Health Problems (continued)

Problem	Symptoms	Causes
Muscular problems	Cramping and spasms of muscles of the limbs and face	Imbalance between calcium and phosphorus
Nervous system disorders	Trembling, paralysis, circling, torticollis, convulsions, death	Various causes: bacterial, viral, parasitic, nutritional, genetic/hereditary
Trauma	Inactivity, lack of appetite, inability to walk or sit normally, broken bones (usually tibia), bleeding, swelling, pain	Many possible types of injuries: bite wounds, being dropped or stepped on, broken bones, broken teeth

*Always consult your veterinarian about all health problems!

and both can produce unwanted side effects. Your pet's treatment will be customized based on its health and the seriousness of its condition and may include special shampoos, ointments, or medication.

Chinchillas are very sensitive to heat and high humidity and can suffer from heatstroke.

Fur chewing: Some chinchillas pull out their fur. They may pull out small patches over a period of time or remove half the fur in their coat overnight. The reasons for this behavior are not clear. Boredom, stress, poor diet, skin infections, environment, hormones, nervousness, and genetics have all been suggested as possible causes. Fur chewing is also associated with thyroid and adrenal gland hyperactivity and low body temperature.

Fur slip (fur throw): When chinchillas are stressed, they shed or throw their fur. The fur can slip off in surprisingly large amounts and ruin the coat. The best way to prevent fur slip is to prevent stress and handle your pet with care by holding it by the base of the tail and not grabbing the skin or fur directly.

Cotton fur syndrome: Excessive levels of protein in the diet (about twice the level normally recom-

What to Do*

See veterinarian for injection of calcium gluconate, and correct dietary deficiency

Treat according to specific diagnosis

Observe closely, determine extent of injury, isolate from other pets, give medication for pain as needed; injuries may require surgical repair

mended) can cause hair fibers to become weak and wavy. This condition can be corrected by returning to a balanced diet. However, the coat will take a long time to regain its normal appearance.

Fatty acid deficiency: Chinchillas need essential fatty acids for healthy skin and coat. Fatty acid deficiency can cause areas of dry, flaky skin and patchy hair loss and skin ulcers. If left untreated, the condition can become severe and lead to death.

Pantothenic acid deficiency: Animals suffering from a deficiency in pantothenic acid are in poor condition, are underweight, and have no appetite. The dull, pale, patchy coat sheds easily and the skin is thick and flaky. Pantothenic acid deficiency may be a cause of stunted growth.

Heatstroke

Chinchillas evolved in cold country. They are heavily furred. So understandably, they can tolerate cold weather better than warm weather and they overheat easily. Chinchillas are comfortable at 65 to 70°F (18 to 21°C). When the temperature rises above 80°F (26.6°C), though, they quickly start to overheat. They suffer even more if the humidity is also high.

A chinchilla suffering from heatstroke drools, lies down, and stretches out in an attempt to cool down. Breathing is rapid, mucous membranes change from a normal pink color to bright red, the ear veins swell, and the ears may redden. In a very short time, the chinchilla becomes weak, unresponsive, dehydrated, and eventually comatose. Without immediate emergency treatment, it dies. If your chinchilla is suffering from heatstroke, you must quickly and safely drop your pet's temperature and give it fluids to treat dehydration.

To cool down your chinchilla, hold it in your hands in a sink full of tepid-to-cool (not cold) water. Do not use ice or ice water because a rapid drop in temperature change can cause your pet to have seizures. Be sure to keep your chinchilla's head above water so it can safely breathe and does not aspirate water into its lungs.

When your chin has regained consciousness, dry it gently and place it into a dry, dark, comfortable cage to rest, and give it fluids. Make sure your pet is fully conscious and able to swallow, so that the fluid does not go into the lungs.

Follow-up care from your veterinarian is absolutely necessary.

You can keep your pet's coat beautiful by careful handling to prevent fur slip and by daily observation to look for early signs of skin and coat problems.

To prevent heatstroke, be sure that your pet's cage is not in direct sunlight. Make sure it is not close to a woodstove, fireplace, radiator, or heater.

High humidity adds to the problem. Heat and high humidity are a deadly combination for chinchillas, so be especially vigilant on hot, humid days. If the weather is too hot

Take Care of That Spine!

In the spine alone, chinchillas have seven cervical vertebrae (bones in the neck), 13 thoracic vertebrae (from which spring 13 pairs of ribs!), six bones in the lumbar spine, two bones in the sacrum, and 23 tailbones. That is a lot of bones that can be potentially broken or injured. Spinal injuries are not unusual, so handle your pet carefully and do not let it fall!

and humid for you, it is much worse for your chinchilla. Keep your pet indoors and turn on the air-conditioning!

When you must transport your chinchilla, never leave it in the car. On a warm day, a car can heat up to 120°F (48.9°C) in a few minutes, even with the windows partially open. Give special consideration to the number of chinchillas you are housing or transporting together. Their combined body heat can be surprising. Whether you have one chinchilla or 100, adequate ventilation is absolutely necessary to help prevent heatstroke.

Broken Bones

Small animals have a way of sometimes being in the wrong place at the wrong time. If your chinchilla is dropped, stepped on, attacked by the family dog or cat, or injured in any way, try to determine how seriously it is hurt and if any bones are broken. Handle your pet gently and carefully until it can be examined by your veterinarian.

The most common fracture or break seen in chinchillas is that of the long bone of the hind leg. In many animals the femur (the leg bone that connects at the hip) is the longest leg bone. However, in the chinchilla, the tibia (the bone that is situated between the foot and the femur) is the longest bone in the leg. The long tibia makes it possible for a chinchilla to leap and bound. The tibia is a very thin, fragile bone that fractures easily. Fractures can be caused by something as simple as catching a leg between the wire mesh of the cage or by improperly restraining the animal by a hind limb. Chinchillas can also break their tibias when they are excited or panicked and ricocheting off hard objects, especially if they have escaped and are loose in the house.

Repairing the tibia and limiting the chinchilla's activity while the bone is healing are difficult. Sometimes the tibia does not heal straight or heal back together at all. However, if treated quickly and properly, the bones can heal and the animal can live a normal life.

If you think your chinchilla has broken its leg, place your pet into a clean, comfortable cage, do not handle it more than necessary, and contact your veterinarian right away. The sooner the break is splinted, the faster and better it will mend.

Pododermatitis

Pododermatitis (inflamed, sore feet, also known as pressure sores) is caused by housing chinchillas on wire mesh floors or sharp, abrasive bedding material. The bottoms of your pet's feet can become tender and sore from walking on rough, irritating surfaces with no place to rest their feet.

A solid cage bottom, comfortable bedding on wire floors, or a footrest (brick, board, or large, flat rock) will prevent this problem. Make sure all bedding material is always clean and dry.

Neurological Problems

Lymphocytic choriomeningitis virus: This virus is spread in the urine of infected rodents, by contact, and by biting insects. Lymphocytic choriomeningitis causes convulsions and death. It is a common disease of mice and hamsters that has been reported in chinchillas. The disease is contagious to humans and causes meningitis and flu-like symptoms. There is no treatment.

Seizures have numerous causes. Chinchillas are very sensitive and susceptible to bacterial infections caused by *Listeria monocytogenes*, which is one cause of neurological disease. Affected chinchillas cannot balance, will circle about, and will convulse. The disease is very serious in chinchillas and almost always ends in death. Genetic (inherited) factors are also important causes of seizures, as in the case of the ruby-eyed gene. Heatstroke, trauma, and poisonings can cause seizures, as will low blood levels of calcium, glucose (sugar), or thiamine. Chinchillas that have eaten hay contaminated by raccoon feces may become infected with the nematode (roundworm) parasite *Baylisascaris procyonis*. This parasite affects the brain and spinal cord and causes loss of balance, torticollis (head tilt), seizures, and paralysis.

Seizures can range in severity from violent convulsions and rigidity to shivering, twitching, paddling, or circling. They may last a few seconds or a few minutes. The more severe, frequent, and longer the seizures, the more serious they are for your pet's health. Animals are exhausted after they have a seizure. Allow your pet to rest in subdued lighting in a comfortable place, and contact your veterinarian for advice.

If the cause of the seizure can be determined (for example, poisoning from eating moldy hay, parasites from eating fecal-contaminated hay,

or poor sanitary conditions leading to exposure to *Listeria* or *Streptococcus*), then you can prevent seizures in the future by eliminating the problem. However, if the cause of the seizure is unknown (idiopathic) or cannot be cured (for example, seizures that are hereditary), then all you can do is keep your pet from injuring itself during a seizure, keep it comfortable after the seizure, and allow it to rest and recover in peace.

Animals with idiopathic epilepsy should not be used for breeding because the condition might be passed on genetically to the offspring.

Reproductive problems are discussed in "Raising Chinchillas."

First Aid Supplies

Here is a list of items to keep in your chinchilla emergency first aid kit, just in case!
- Your veterinarian's phone number
- The phone number of the nearest emergency pet hospital
- The phone number of the Animal Poison Control Center
- Mild laxative (Laxatone)
- Hair ball treatment (Petramalt)
- Electrolyte solution (available from your veterinarian, or Pedialyte)
- Small syringe (for feeding or enemas)
- Mineral oil
- Vegetable oil
- Small forceps
- Eye ointment
- Gauze (to make a small sling to open mouth)

Zoonotic Diseases

Zoonotic diseases are diseases that can be shared between animals and humans. Many species of animals are carriers of certain diseases that do not make them ill but can make people very sick. Likewise, people can carry germs to which they are resistant but that can make some animals sick. Some germs cause illness in both humans and animals.

Chinchillas can have infections contagious to humans:

1. Lymphocytic choriomeningitis (LCM) virus

2. Ringworm: *Trichophyton mentagrophytes* and *Microsporum canis*

3. Bacteria: *Listeria monocytogenes*

4. Protozoa: *Toxoplasmosis, Giardia*, and *Cryptosporidium*

5. Various gastrointestinal bacteria

Wash your hands well before and after handling your chinchilla. If your pet is sick, your physician and veterinarian can answer questions you may have about contagion.

When Is Surgery Necessary?

Chinchillas do not make good surgical candidates. They are high-risk patients because they are easily stressed and do not tolerate restraint, anesthesia, or surgery as well as many other pets. Unless it is absolutely necessary, your chinchilla should avoid the operating room!

Unfortunately, for some health problems, surgery is the best or only choice. Here is a list of some chinchilla health conditions that are best treated surgically:

- Uterine infection (pyometra)
- Dystocia (difficulty delivering kits through the birth canal)
- Retained, dead fetus that cannot pass naturally
- Intestinal obstruction, impaction, intussusception
- Repair of broken bones
- Certain kinds of dental procedures

Should Your Chinchilla Be Neutered?

Neutering refers to the removal of some, or all, of the tissues in the body associated with reproduction (testicles in the male, ovaries and uterus in the female). Neutering in the chinchilla is accomplished surgically.

Most pet chinchillas do not need to be neutered. However, if you have a male and a female and want to house them together but do not want them to breed, then neutering is a possible alternative (assuming they are compatible!).

Deciding whether to have the male castrated or the female spayed (a term for an ovariohysterectomy, or removal of the ovaries and uterus) is an important decision because there is always a degree of risk with any surgery and anesthesia, even in the most expert hands. As a rule, castra-

Dust baths are very important and necessary for good grooming.

tion is a less invasive and a shorter procedure than an ovariohysterectomy, and recovery time is less.

Be sure the veterinarian you select to do the procedure has clinical and surgical experience with chinchillas!

Grooming

Keeping your chinchilla's coat in tip-top condition is easy! Just allow it to have a dust bath at least once or twice a week and comb out the loose, shedding hair once a week. Pet suppliers sell chinchilla combs. However, you can also use a fine-toothed comb, such as a flea comb, in combination with a wider-spaced tooth comb (for rabbits) and a gentle, stiff-bristle brush. Comb the fur gen-

tly against the grain to separate the hairs and give your pet's coat a full, plush appearance. For the finishing touch, take a pair of small scissors and gently trim the tips of the stray hairs on the tuft of your chinchilla's hair.

Some chinchilla owners bathe their pets when the fur is light colored or has stains that are difficult to remove by dust bathing only. Most chinchillas do not like being wet, and baths flatten the coat down and make it appear less fluffy. If you decide to bathe your pet, follow these simple guidelines:

1. Use a gentle, emollient (non-soap) shampoo.

2. *Do not use flea shampoos or products that contain pesticides; they can be harmful for chinchillas.*

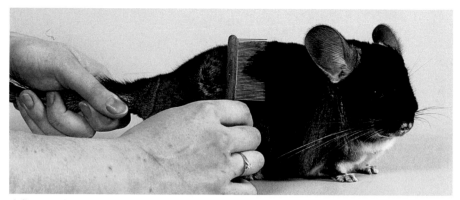

A fine-toothed comb separates the fur and makes it more voluminous. Be gentle when you handle and comb your pet so that you do not damage its coat.

3. Make sure the water is lukewarm, not hot.

4. *Never leave your chinchilla alone in the bath!*

5. Dry your pet completely with a soft towel, and do not allow it to get chilled or cold.

6. Keep your pet out of drafts.

7. If drying your pet with a hair dryer (this method is suitable only for very tame chinchillas that are not easily frightened), be sure the air is not too hot and does not burn your pet's sensitive skin.

8. Let your chin take a dust bath as soon as it is dry.

9. *Do not bathe your chinchilla within two weeks of showing it!* Its fur will not look nice and plush.

10. If your pet is frightened and does not want to be bathed, do not bathe it!

Dusting is the best and most natural way for your pet to stay clean. Dusting powder lasts a long time and can be reused often. However, if it is soiled, it should be discarded.

The Senior Chinchilla

Chinchillas typically live a long time. They deserve kind care and consideration in their golden years. It might surprise you that geriatric chin-

To groom your chinchilla, use a soft brush to fluff out the fur.

Senior chinchillas need a safe, cozy, quiet place to rest and feel secure in their golden years.

chillas need a lot of the same things baby chinchillas do: comfortable housing, easy-to-digest high-calorie foods, soft bedding, and a stress-free environment.

Senior chinchillas need to be monitored closely to make sure they are comfortable. Their body does not work as well as it used to. Just like baby kits, older chinchillas need to be kept warm (not hot!) or cool, depending on the ambient tempera-ture, because they do not ther-moregulate (regulate their body temperature) well. Older chinchillas, like older people, suffer from arthritis; stiff joints; brittle, fragile bones; and weaker, smaller muscles. They do

not absorb nutrients as well as they once did and lose weight easily.

Watch your chinchilla closely, and care for it according to its needs. Something as simple as soft bedding and easy-to-digest foods can make all the difference in improving your pet's quality of life.

Euthanasia: The Hardest Decision of All

Even with the best care in the world, your chinchilla will someday develop signs of old age or illness.

This will be a difficult time for your pet, because it will not be able to run, play, and enjoy life as it did when it was younger and healthy. It will also be an emotionally painful time for you. You will feel helpless in your inability to prevent or cure the problem, and you will not want your small friend to suffer for a moment. At some point in time you will ask the question: Should my pet be euthanized?

Euthanasia means putting an animal to death humanely, peacefully, and painlessly. There are different ways veterinarians euthanize animals, depending on the circumstances. Euthanasia is usually done by first giving the animal a sedative to make it sleep deeply and then giving it a lethal substance by injection that ends its life almost instantly.

It seems like there is no "right time" for euthanasia. For most people, it seems like it is either done too early or too late. If you worry that perhaps your pet might have been able to enjoy a few extra days of life, you may think euthanasia was done too early. If your pet is suffering and you wish you had taken action sooner, it seems like euthanasia was done too late. You are not alone in these feelings.

The truth is, if you are asking yourself whether your chinchilla should be euthanized, there must be good reasons. The decision of when to euthanize is a difficult one that depends upon many things. A good guide is if your pet's suffering cannot be relieved, if its quality of life is poor, or if the bad days simply outnumber the good days, then it is time to consider euthanasia seriously. Your veterinarian can answer any specific questions you or your family may have. Your veterinarian can also help you if you wish to find a pet cemetery or have your pet cremated.

During this emotional time, remember to take care of yourself and allow time to grieve. If you have children in the family, deal with the issue of animal loss at a level they can understand, comfort them, and let them share their sadness. Take comfort in the knowledge you took good care of your pet throughout its life and that you made the best decisions regarding its health and welfare, even when you had to make the most difficult decision of all.

A necropsy (animal autopsy) and diagnostic workup is highly recommended for any animal that has a sudden or unexplained death. This is especially true if other chinchillas have been exposed to it or a zoonotic disease (a disease transmissible between animals and humans) is suspected.

Chapter Nine

Raising Chinchillas

Chinchillas are so much fun and kits are so cute that at some time you might consider raising them as a hobby. If you want to raise chinchillas, getting off to a good start and doing it correctly right from the beginning are very important. That means learning as much as you can about chinchilla behavior and reproduction and observing your animals closely. Raising chinchillas is not simply a matter of putting two animals together in a cage. It requires knowledge and good judgment. You must know which animals compliment each other and are the best match, which are most likely to produce quality offspring, and which are compatible. In addition, you must be prepared for emergency situations and medical conditions associated with pregnancy, lactation, or perinatal care. Keep some funds in reserve in case surgery (such as a cesarean section) or medications are needed. Raising chinchillas can be a lot of fun, but it can also be very costly. Think about why you want to raise chinchillas, and make sure your expectations are reasonable.

Females can be aggressive and injure males. Make sure individuals are compatible before housing them together.

Reasons for Raising Chinchillas

If you are interested in raising chinchillas for exhibition, breeding stock, or fur, be forewarned! It is a competitive world out there, and your hobby will take a lot of time and be very expensive. If you think you can make money selling chinchillas as pets, think again! If the sale of your pets pays for the expenses of raising them, you will be very lucky indeed, but it is highly unlikely that you will turn a profit.

If you want to raise chinchillas to make an income by selling their pelts, you will definitely need guidance from successful fur farmers experienced in this competitive and unpredictable market. (This handbook is written for pet owners. Therefore, methods for selecting, feeding, housing, and raising "herds" of chinchillas on a large scale for the fur industry are not discussed in this book. Books and resources that give detailed information on raising chinchillas for pelts are included in "Useful Addresses and Literature.")

Raising chinchillas for exhibition and breeding stock can be very

Are you considering raising chinchillas as a hobby? Think twice! Breeding chinchillas is hard work and expensive—and there is a lot to learn before you begin.

others who have been deeply involved in chinchillas long before you considered breeding them as a hobby.

Remember that the goal of a good chinchilla breeder is to produce healthier, hardier, and more beautiful animals with good dispositions and less genetic problems with each successive generation. These "simple goals" are not as easy to attain as one might think. So get ready for lots of homework and hard work—and fun!

Chinchilla Reproduction

rewarding, but unless you raise chinchillas on a very grand scale and make significant investments in time and money along the way, you are not likely to make a profit, let alone earn a living.

Your main reasons for raising chinchillas should be dedication to improving the overall quality of the animal, learning more, sharing the information you have learned with others, and having a good time in the process. Of course, you cannot get started without the help of an experienced chinchilla breeder because you will be launching your breeding program from the previous efforts of

One of the most interesting facts about chinchilla reproduction is that the chinchilla has a relatively long gestation period (duration of pregnancy) compared with other rodents or even compared with other animals. Gestation in the *C. laniger* lasts 105 to 118 days (and up to 128 days for *C. brevicaudata*), with an average of 111 days. As a comparison, hamsters have a gestation period of 16 to 18 days, and a much large animal, the pig, has the same gestation period of 111 days!

Chinchillas also reach sexual maturity much later than many rodents. Although puberty may start as early as five and a half months of age, many chinchillas do not reach sexual maturity until eight months of age. A mouse reaches sexual maturity at six weeks of age!

Chinchillas are seasonal breeders and do not reproduce year-round. Small litter size is another interesting chinchilla characteristic. Unlike rats, hamsters, and mice, chinchillas do not have large litters. Although they can have from one to six babies in a litter, most chinchillas average only two babies in a litter. In other words, you wait a long time for a very few number of precious babies. Chinchillas are not animals of mass production.

What does all this mean to you as a budding chinchilla breeder? For one thing, you need to pay close attention to your animals so you will know when to plan for a litter. You also need to recognize that you will not be making a fortune off the sale of large numbers of kits. Most chinchilla hobbyists raise a litter because they have plans to keep one or more of the kits as a pet, to show, or to add to their breeding program. However, if you are planning on selling your kits, make sure that you have good homes lined up for them *before* you breed the parents.

If you do not want your chinchillas to breed, separate the males from the females at the time of weaning. Same-sex chin siblings will live together peacefully if you keep them housed together from the time they are weaned.

Reproductive Characteristics

Chinchillas have some very interesting and unusual reproductive characteristics.

Chinchilla babies are precocious. They are born fully furred, with their teeth erupted and eyes wide open.

The female chinchilla has six nipples. One pair is located in the inguinal area, and two pairs are located along the sides of the thorax (called lateral thoracic nipples). The position of the nipples makes it possible for the mother to huddle the kits and for them to lie on their backs while they suckle. (Note: Some pet books state the chinchilla has eight nipples. This is not in keeping with the scientific literature or the author's observations.)

The chinchilla has a bicornate uterus and a double cervix (opening to the uterus). That means that from the cervix, the uterus branches into a Y shape, consisting of a left and a right uterine horn. This conformation enables the mother to carry more than one offspring in each of the uterine horns.

All female mammals are born with a vaginal membrane that remains closed until puberty (sexual maturity) is reached. In the chinchilla, this membrane opens during estrus, when mating takes place, and then closes again. This process can take place within 12 hours but usually takes two to four days. The vaginal membrane opens again before parturition (birth) and closes after birth or after mating on the postpartum (time immediately after birth) estrus. Do not allow your chinchilla to breed during the postpartum estrus because she will have the double difficulty of feeding her kits while a new litter is developing inside her body. This is quite a heavy demand on a small animal! It is great for perpetuating the species, but it is tough on the individual animal!

If mating does not take place on the postpartum estrus, the female chinchilla will come into estrus later when she weans her kits (a minimum of 56 days later, usually longer). This is called the postlactation estrus. Again, hold off on breeding your chinchilla rather than breeding her on the postlactation estrus, when she will already have depleted a lot of her energy stores and body fat coping with raising a litter of kits. She may not be completely recovered or in top condition, and another pregnancy so soon after lactation can be quite stressful and hard on her. People who breed their animals so soon are usually doing so to maximize production, as in the fur industry. Eventually this takes its toll on the animal. This type of breeding schedule is not recommended for pets.

Even if a mating does take place, it does not guarantee a pregnancy. A female chinchilla may mate but not conceive during the postpartum or postlactation estrus. All of the reasons for a failure to conceive are not known but may have to do with the female's inability to handle the extra stress at that time. Sometimes a female will become pregnant but not carry the pregnancy to term (completion) and the fetuses will be resorbed.

Kits can have a tough time as well, especially if their mother is stressed and not able to produce enough milk to feed them adequately. Sometimes kits do not survive during the lactation period (the time they are receiving milk from their mother). If the babies die during this time, the mother can quickly return to estrus again.

This is also a postlactation estrus and is nature's way of keeping chinchillas pregnant and reproducing, a sort of species survival tactic.

The presence of chinchillas in estrus can bring other chinchillas into estrus. An old breeder's trick is to house female chinchillas that are not yet in estrus near a female currently in estrus. This stimulates the nonestrous females to come into estrus sooner, probably through olfactory signals and pheromones. By stimulating estrus in this manner, chinchilla farmers can maximize chinchilla reproduction.

Males are easy to identify. They are usually smaller than females and have a spread of bare skin between the penis and the anus. The penis is covered by small spines, is directed posteriorly (backward), and has an S-shaped bend to it. This bend straightens out when breeding takes place. Do not be alarmed if you observe the penis in its straightened state, in which case it can reach as far as the axillary region (armpit) of the animal, a distance of more than 4 inches (11 cm).

The testicles of male chinchillas are retained inguinally or in the abdominal cavity. There is no scrotum. The tail of the epidiymis is contained within a post-anal sac.

Upon ejaculation (the release of sperm during breeding), the secretions of reproductive accessory glands mix with the semen and form a mixture that forms a small plug resembling a small, whitish sack with a pungent smell. This is a copulatory plug (some breeders call it a stopper). It may be visible at the entry to the female's vagina shortly after breeding or in the bedding of the cage. The copulatory plug is a useful indicator that mating has occurred. However, it is not always easy to find. So if you cannot locate it in the cage, do not assume that the female was not bred.

Breeding Methods and Housing

There are several kinds of breeding methods. The one you use will determine how you house your chinchillas and how many chinchillas you raise.

A good breeding facility is clean and well-ventilated. Animals are identified by cage cards or ear tags and breeding records are accurate and up to date.

Pair Mating

In this method, a single male and female are housed together and allowed to breed. Pair mating works well for the beginner who is starting off with just one or a few pairs of animals. Animal numbers are low, and production is slow using this method. It is ideal for the hobbyist who just wants to raise a few animals each year.

Breeding Runs

This method is the one most commonly used by big chinchilla ranchers. However, it is simple enough for the novice. Six to eight cages, each containing one female chinchilla, are attached in a row. The backs of the cages have an opening large enough for a male chinchilla to enter and exit. A main enclosed runway spans the distance behind the cages so that the male may enter or exit any female's cage at will and breed her. The female wears a light aluminum collar that is wide enough to prevent her from exiting the opening at the back of her cage. This way the male can come and go as he pleases, breed any females in estrus, and escape from an aggressive female, and females cannot leave their cages and fight with each other. It is the best of all worlds for the male! Besides that, it is an excellent way to breed several females to an outstanding male and rapidly increase the quality and size of the herd.

Colony Caging

Colony caging is a little trickier and riskier than the other methods because it requires closer observation and fast action. When using this method, several females are placed together in a very large cage with a single male. Animals must be closely observed for compatibility. If fighting takes place, they must be separated immediately. Chinchilla ranchers use this method as a way to bring females into estrus by exposing them to scents (and pheromones) of other females that are in estrus. As soon as a female is bred, she must be relocated to a new cage and housed alone. This method is used by experienced chinchilla breeders and is not recommended for the novice breeder.

Reproductive Cycle

Chinchillas are seasonal breeders. This means that they do not reproduce year-round. This seasonality is due to the female's estrous cycle, because males remain fertile year-round.

In the southern hemisphere, where chinchillas originated, they breed from May to November. In the northern hemisphere, their reproductive cycle is shifted six months to accommodate the difference in seasons, light cycle, and climate, and they breed from November to May. Although female chinchillas ovulate (release eggs from the ovaries) about once a month (every 38 days), they usually produce only two litters a year.

Female animals are generally classified into two groups. Spontaneous ovulators are animals that ovulate spontaneously, whether mated or not. (Examples include hamsters and mice.) Induced ovulators are animals that ovulate in response to mating. (Examples include cats, ferrets, and rabbits.) Chinchillas are unusual in that they are a blend of both. Most chinchillas ovulate spontaneously, but they will also ovulate in response to being mated.

Estrus

Estrus is the time during the breeding season, just before and just after ovulation, during which the female will permit the male to mate with her. Estrus in the chinchilla usually lasts from 12 hours to two days.

It is characterized by a change in color around the perineal area from pink to deep red. Swelling of the vulva does not usually occur, although the reddened tissue may make it appear that way.

As a chinchilla breeder, you need to observe your animals closely, particularly during the breeding season. This will allow you to know when to put the female and male together and make plans for the litter well in advance of the birth.

Puberty

Unlike many rodents, chinchillas take a long time to reach sexual maturity. They may reach puberty as early as five and a half months of age, but the average is about eight months of age. Male chinchillas are usually smaller than the females and need extra time to attain the size and physical development to be able to breed successfully. However, they may produce sperm as early as two months of age.

Courtship Behavior

During the breeding season, the male chinchilla will initiate courtship by grooming the female. As the courting ritual continues, the male will attempt to mount the female. If she is not yet receptive, her behavior can be unpredictable. Females can be very aggressive toward males, even during estrus. It is extremely rare, though, for a male to fight back or even attempt to protect himself other than to run away in panic from the female. So you must closely supervise the animals to make sure the female does not harm the male. Some females are so much larger, stronger, and aggressive than the males that they have been known to kill the males, especially if the males have no way to escape from them.

Several breedings may take place at intervals, but all take place quickly, probably as an antipredator defense mechanism. If breeding took too long, chinchillas would be vulnerable to predators in the area.

Ovulation

Ovulation is the release of eggs from the ovaries. Assuming the male is fertile, the number of young conceived will depend upon the number of viable (live, healthy) eggs released during ovulation. Litter size ranges from one to six, with an average of two.

Implantation

Implantation, the attachment of the embryo to the uterus, takes place in the chinchilla at five days after mating. The placenta is an organ that is part of the baby and not of the mother. Each individual fetus has a placenta of its own. The placenta attaches each kit to the mother's uterus so that it can receive nutrition through the blood supply. Different animal species have different kinds of placentation. Chinchillas have a chorioallantoic-type placentation.

Even though embryos may attach to the uterus, things can go wrong and pregnancies may not be carried to term, or completion. Fetal reab-

Baby chinchillas are born with their eyes open and fully furred, but they still need their mother's care and milk until they are at least six to eight weeks of age.

sorption is common in chinchillas at any stage of their pregnancy and is observed more often than fetal mummification or abortion.

Pregnancy

The time during which the female is pregnant, that is, from conception to birth, is called gestation. The 111-day (105- to 118-day range) gestation period in the chinchilla is very long compared with most rodents. Chinchilla fetuses grow more slowly than most rodent fetuses of closely related species.

Usually a long gestation means the offspring are born precocious, that is, well developed and fully able to fend for themselves. Although chinchillas are born with fur and their eyes open, they still need their mother for protection and nutrition for at least six to eight weeks.

An interesting theory has been postulated to account for long gestation periods in some hystricomorph rodents such as the chinchilla. It suggests that species with long life spans and long reproductive periods have large brains at birth and in adulthood and that the gestation length is determined by the brain weight and stage of development at birth.

If your chinchilla is carrying several young, you will probably detect an increase in size in her abdomen during the last month of her pregnancy, and when you pick her up you may notice she feels heavier. You should weigh her weekly to keep track of any unusual fluctuations in body weight that could signal a problem.

Handle your pregnant chinchilla carefully and gently so the unborn babies are not crushed or injured. Do

Reproductive Facts

Breeding season—males	Fertile year-round
Breeding season—females 　In northern hemisphere 　In southern hemisphere	Seasonal November to May May to November
Estrous cycle	Every 38 days
Duration of estrus	12 hours to 4 days
Induced ovulator	Yes
Spontaneous ovulator	Yes
Implantation	5½ days after fertilization takes place
Gestation	111 days (105 to 118 days) *C. laniger* Up to 128 days *C. brevicaudata*
Litter size	Average 2 (1 to 6)
Litters per year	Can have up to 3 if bred continuously during breeding season (not recommended)
Breed in postpartum estrus	Yes
Breed in postlactation estrus	Yes
Weight at birth	1 to 2 ounces (30 to 60 g)
Born with fur and eyes open	Yes
Weaning	6 to 8 weeks of age
Sexual maturity (puberty)	5¼ to 8 months of age

not grasp the mother-to-be too firmly around her abdomen. Support her body when you hold her. Do not make changes in her cage that might upset her. Make sure newspaper or soft bedding is on the cage floor so that when the kits are born they cannot catch their small feet and limbs in the wire mesh cage floor.

Birth (Partuition)

Birth usually takes place in the morning hours. Chinchillas give birth by sitting up and hunching over, or squatting. Kits are usually born a few minutes apart, although the time interval between kits can be as long as an hour. Some kits are born head first, others may be born breech (hind limbs and rump first). The placenta passes shortly after the kits. There should be one placenta for each kit. It is normal for the mother to eat the placenta.

If your chinchilla has been in labor for more than an hour, if the kit is partway through the birth canal and the mother is unable to pass it, or if the placentas have not passed, contact your veterinarian immediately.

Kits weigh about 2 ounces (60 g) at birth, although they may be as small as 1 ounce (30 g). During the birth process and afterwards, the mother and her babies may chirp softly to one another. If you listen closely, you will recognize these tender sounds as the announcement of the birth of a new litter!

Chinchilla parents are very protective of their young. It is unlikely, but possible, that the mother will bite you if you reach into the cage, so be careful! Be sensitive to her feelings. If she is upset, she will growl or snarl. If she is very fearful, she will make the eek eek cry. During the first few hours after birth, it is best to leave the new family alone.

Mortality can be as high as 10 percent at birth. When it doubt, do not hesitate to contact your veterinarian for help.

Soon after birth, the female chinchilla will come into estrus again. This is called a postpartum estrus. This early estrus is not uncommon in rodent species. If your chinchilla does not breed and conceive on the postpartum estrus, she may return to estrus again (postlactation estrus) when the kits are weaned. If bred, she could conceive at that time.

Parental Care

In the wild, parental care begins long before the babies are born. It begins as a bond between the parents that ensures the two are compatible and will breed, raise, and protect the litter together. Some male chinchillas tolerate their babies, sit with them, and are very protective of them. Unlike many hystricomorph rodents, father chinchillas do not enurinate (spray urine on) their mates or on the kits. Males that accept their young probably do so because the babies smell similar to their mother due to their close contact with her.

Unfortunately, not all males are kind to their babies. Some can be aggressive and kill them. Unless you are absolutely positive about the gentle, paternal nature of your male chinchilla, you should remove him from the cage before your female gives birth. If the female is aggressive to the male, it is best, and safest, to remove him from the cage shortly after mating takes place.

In some cases, if the male is separated from the female and the rest of the family, he will be depressed and go off his feed. It is important to know your animals and their personalities and compatibilities very well and observe them closely to prevent accident, injury, fighting, or depression among them.

Mother chinchillas take good care of their kits and can raise them alone, without the assistance of the father. The babies depend on their mother for nutrition, warmth, and protection.

Lactation

Lactation is the production of milk by the mammary glands, or breasts. The composition of milk, its percentage of fat, protein, and water, varies for each species. Lactation is a unique feature of all mammals. It allows mother animals to nourish their immature young safely in hiding, any time, anywhere. It is a practical approach to increase survival of offspring during times of food shortage.

When a mother is lactating, she is turning the food she has eaten and the fat she has stored into milk for her kits and body heat to keep them warm. This process requires energy and burns up calories. The mother has to eat and drink a lot more than usual.

Kits depend on their mothers for survival. She will nurse them by huddling over them. In a huddling position, the mother drapes herself over the kits. Babies may lie on their backs underneath their mother to suckle. As the kits grow larger, they may suckle on their stomachs or sit-

Not a "Homemaker"!
Chinchillas are not nestbuilders or homemakers like most rodents. Your chinchilla will probably simply have her babies on the cage floor. The only sign of impending birth that you might observe is that she may act more nervous, animated, or agitated shortly before she goes into labor. Be sure your female is in a maternity cage— a cage with a solid-bottom floor or a floor well covered with bedding so that it is soft for the new arrivals. Make sure wire mesh is small enough that the kits cannot get their feet and limbs trapped and injured in it. Wire mesh should be less than $\frac{1}{2} \times \frac{1}{2}$ inch (approximately 1×1 cm).

ting up. Eventually, when they grow stronger, they may force their mother onto her side while she nurses them.

Lactation lasts about six to eight weeks. Kits should not be weaned before that time. In order for a kit to survive, it must suckle at least until the age of 25 days. Even though survival may be possible for an animal weaned so young, it is not recommended. Kits need mother's milk for at least twice that long.

Mother chinchillas can lose a lot of weight during lactation, especially if they do not receive enough good food or have too many babies to nurse. As the kits grow, so do their nutritional demands and the demands on their mother's body to produce milk. Be sure to give your mother chinchilla lots of nutritious food and unlimited water during lactation.

Growth and Survival

Newborn chinchillas average about 2 ounces (60 g) in weight. The size of the kit is inversely proportional to the size of the litter. This means that the more kits in the litter, the smaller each individual kit is. In other words, kits from a litter size of two will usually be larger than kits from a litter of three, four, five, or six individuals.

Chinchilla growth is slow compared with most rodents. Kits gain 0.126 ounces (3.6 g) daily during the first month of life. That is a total of more than 6 ounces (180 g) of weight gain in the first month. From the second month of age until six months of age, youngsters gain about 0.05 ounces (1.56 g) daily. From six months of age until one year of age, chinchillas gain 0.022 ounces (0.65 g) daily. As you can see, chinchillas do not reach their full adult weight and development until they are about one year of age.

- Male chinchillas may be used for breeding as early as six months of age if they are strong, mature, large enough, and physically capable.
- Female chinchillas should not be used for breeding until they are at least eight months of age and not until they are mature enough and physically able to deal with the pregnancy.
- Females should not weigh less than a pound (600 g) when they are first bred.
- Females should be bred before two years of age. Otherwise they may have difficulty reproducing or may never reproduce.

Chinchillas take a long time to grow up. They do not reach adult weight and development until they are about one year of age.

Weaning

A weaned animal is an animal that no longer requires and is no longer receiving nourishment from its mother's milk. Chinchilla kits can run and play the day of birth and take a real interest in solid food, especially about a week from birth. Nevertheless, they cannot survive without their mother's milk and need to have it until at least three and a half weeks of age in order to survive.

Survival rates by the time of weaning are often as low as 75 percent. Kits should not be weaned from their mother earlier than six to eight weeks of age.

• Before breeding your female chinchilla, check to be sure that her pelvis is large enough to allow passage of baby chinchillas' large heads through the birth canal. This can be done by lifting the female's tail and pressing in the area of the pelvis where you can feel a circular indentation. The circular area should be at least an inch (2.54 cm) in diameter. Pelvic size can also be confirmed by radiography (X ray).

Imprinting and Taming

Imprinting is what takes place when a very young animal sees another animal and immediately forms a close bond with it. In the wild, baby animals almost always imprint on their mothers. She is the first thing they see, smell, hear, and recognize. They depend on her for protection. They follow her and learn from her. The same is true for chinchillas. By the time you are able to handle the kits safely, they will have already imprinted on their mother.

This in no way interferes with your ability to tame your kit. Baby chins are very gentle animals that are curious and easy to tame. All that is required of you is the fun job of handling your kits regularly! Kits quickly turn into affectionate and enjoyable pets. If their mother is friendly and tame, your job is all the easier because kits get their cues from their mother. If she is tame and enjoys being handled and visiting people,

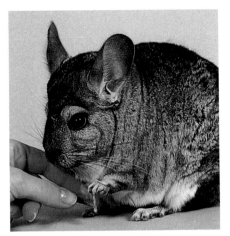

Young chinchillas are easy to tame. Frequent handling and a small, healthy treat now and then help speed up the process.

they will follow their mother's example. The babies will quickly recognize you as a friend and provider of food. The will look forward to your visits.

Sexing the Kits

Determining the sex of the kits at an early age is not difficult. Hold the baby carefully, belly up, with its back against the palm of your hand. You may hold the tail gently at the base, but do not pull on it. Once you have identified the anus, located under the tail, proceed upward to the genital opening. The distance between the anus and the urethral orifice, or the anogenital distance, is greater in males than in females. There is also an expanse of bare skin between the penis and the anus. Females have a small slit opening, no bare skin, and

Male chinchillas have an expanse of bare skin between the penis and the anus.

a shorter distance from the genital opening to the anus. By comparing the littermates with each other and noting the anogenital distance, you will quickly learn to identify the males from the females.

Raising the Babies

Once you wean the young chinchillas, they can be housed just like the adults. They have the same needs: nutritious food, fresh water, an exercise wheel, a dust bath, interest-

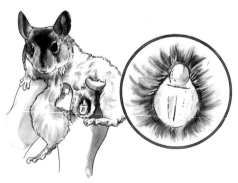

The anogenital distance is shorter in females than in males.

ing toys, a comfortable temperature, and safe, escape-proof housing. Of course, they also need lots of attention from you!

Regular handling is an important part of keeping your pets tame. Young chins are naturally friendly, but they are also quick and active. They have no fear or apparent awareness of heights, so hold on to them carefully so they do not fall.

Kits are also curious and love to investigate. Sometimes they want to explore, and other times they enjoy being held. Your chins will be a continual source of entertainment for you. The more time you spend with them, the friendlier and more fun they will be.

Hand-Feeding Kits

Sometimes the mother chinchilla does not produce enough milk to feed her kits, or she may die, leaving her babies orphaned. If this happens, you have a lot of work ahead of you because you must take over the mother's duties. If you are in the difficult and challenging position of hand-raising newborn kits, be prepared for long, sleepless nights and a small chance of success. Hopefully, you will not encounter these sad situations frequently. On the other hand, the more experience you acquire hand-feeding kits, the more skilled you will be at it. When the babies survive and thrive, you will feel a true sense of reward and accomplishment!

The secrets to hand-feeding kits successfully are small, frequent meals; a wholesome, fresh, warm diet; and lots of patience. *Never try to feed a baby chinchilla too much at one feeding, and never try to feed it faster than it can comfortably swallow.* Both overfeeding and rapid feeding can lead to food aspiration (food being sucked into the trachea and into the lungs), leading to breathing difficulties and pneumonia. When hand-feeding kits, easy does it!

Do not feed your kits milk. It can cause diarrhea and gastric upset.

In the beginning, kits should be fed every two to three hours as needed. They may be fed with an eyedropper or a small syringe (without a needle). As kits grow older, they will lap up their formula directly from a spoon or a very small jar lid. Watch them closely so you will know exactly how much each kit eats, and weigh the kits daily. Keep notes for yourself on their food consumption and weight gain.

Newborn kits can be fed Esbilac for the first few days of life until they are able to consume more solid mixtures. At that time you can add a little bit of oat cereal made for human babies.

Tips for Success

• *Be patient!* The kits take a long time to eat a small amount.
• *Do not overfeed!* Several small meals are safer than fewer large meals. If you see formula coming out of the kit's nostrils, the liquid has probably gone into the lungs. If this happens, the kit may develop pneumonia and die.
• *Do not feed newborn kits cow's milk or products containing cow's*

Emergency Formula for Orphan Chinchillas

• ⅓ ounce (10 g) ground chinchilla pellets (make sure these contain calcium)
• ⅓ ounce (10 g) oat cereal
• ¹⁄₃₀ ounce (1 mL) dextrose (available from your veterinarian)
• ⅙ ounce (5 mL) Pedialyte
• 10 mg vitamin C (available in tablet or liquid form from your pharmacy)
• Bottled water, enough to make a liquid when ingredients are blended

1. Blend thoroughly, and warm the formula to body temperature (do not make it hot!).
2. Use an eyedropper to feed, and feed as much as the kit will eat on its own. Feed slowly, and do not force feed!
3. Make sure the mixture is prepared fresh daily and is fed at body temperature.

milk! These can cause diarrhea and gastric upset.
• *Do not feed chopped vegetables! These can cause choking.*

Make sure the kits do not go too long between feedings and get overly hungry.

In addition to feeding the orphan kits, you will probably have to stimulate them to urinate and defecate after meals. You can do this by taking a warm, damp, cloth and *lightly dabbing* (do not rub!) their anogenital area.

Keep the kits warm (not hot) by placing a heating pad, set at *low heat*, under *half* of their housing area. This way, if they get too warm, they

The main causes of death in kits—cold, dehydration, and low blood sugar—are easy to prevent.

can move to the part of their cage where the floor is not heated. You can also give the kits a warm water bottle (not hot), but you must replace it when it begins to cool so that the babies do not get chilled. *Do not use a heat lamp to warm the kits. If placed too close, it will burn and dehydrate the babies.*

The three main killers of newborn animals are hypothermia (cold), dehydration (not enough fluid intake), and hypoglycemia (low blood sugar due to not eating enough).

If you can keep your kits warm, well hydrated, and well fed, you will be well on your way to saving their lives!

Good-bye Baby

As tempting as it is, you probably will not keep every baby chinchilla you raise. As a responsible breeder,

you will be sure that the youngsters are going to loving homes where they will receive good care.

To be sure everything goes well for the kits, give their new owners as much information as you can about their care. Show them the type of cage you use to house the kits, and demonstrate how to pick up the animals and examine them. Give the new owners a bag of the food you are currently feeding. This will prevent the stress of a change in diet. Finally, in case of a problem, recommend any veterinarians you know who have a special interest in chinchillas.

Reproductive Problems

When you raise chinchillas, you need to have a lot of space for extra cages and housing in case you encounter problems. The more chins you raise, the more likely your chances are of having problems at some time. In fact, breeders that have never encountered reproductive problems with their herds probably just have not been breeding many animals or have not been breeding chinchillas for very long!

As your breeding projects continue, your chinchilla population will increase. You must have plenty of room for all of your animals so they do not become overcrowded, stressed, and ill.

In many situations, you will need additional cages so you can separate your animals. For example, chinchillas are not concerned about family relationships as far as inbreeding or incest is concerned. Siblings must be separated, and mothers must be separated from their sons before they reach sexual maturity. Of course, you will also need housing to separate males from females when you do not want them to breed or fight. If any of your animals are ill, they will need to be isolated from the others so they can recover in peace and quiet. Isolation also prevents the spread of disease if a medical problem is contagious.

As a chinchilla breeder, you may encounter a variety of medical conditions specific to the chinchilla's reproductive system. You need to know how to recognize them in their early stages so you can take immediate action and contact your veterinarian for help.

Dystocia

Dystocia is difficulty giving birth. It does not occur often in chinchillas. When it does, though, it is a serious medical emergency that usually requires surgery to save the mother and kits. If the head of the fetus is too large to pass through the birth canal, the kit will die while it is still inside the uterus or lodged partially in the birth canal. It may eventually pass and be born dead (stillbirth).

This life-threatening condition is more common with young, immature females weighing less than 1 pound or 600 g and those with small pelvic openings, or birth canals. Kits from small litters tend to be larger than those from large litters and have more difficulty passing through the birth canal.

Fetal Resorption

Fetal resorption is when the fetuses die in the uterus and are resorbed back into the mother's body. Fetal resorption is not unusual in chinchillas and is noted more often than abortion, stillbirths (the death and expulsion of the unborn fetus at any stage in development), or mummified fetuses. Not all causes of fetal resorption are known. However, they could be linked to infections (viral or bacterial), inadequate nutrition, or poor health.

Stillbirths

Stillbirth means the kits are born dead. They can be completely developed and ready to be born but have died in the uterus before birth. Stillbirths may go undetected because the mother chinchilla often eats the dead kits.

Mummified Fetuses

If a fetus dies during gestation but is not resorbed, it can dry out and remain in the uterus in a mummified state. Mummified fetuses cause sterility because females carrying mummified fetuses do not become pregnant again until the fetus is removed.

Mastitis

Mastitis is an inflammation, infection, caking, or hardening of the mammary glands. Mastitis interferes with or stops milk production.

Metritis and Pyometra

Bacteria and retained placentas and fetuses can cause metritis (inflammation of the uterus) and pyometra (serious infections of the uterus) that can lead to the death of the female. Pus may accumulate in the uterus. A foul-smelling vaginal discharge may be noted, and the female runs a fever, stops eating, stops lactating, and quickly debilitates. Successful treatment of uterine infections is difficult. The best option is usually to remove the uterus and ovaries (ovariohysterectomy) in addition to giving antibiotics. The decision to do surgery must be made quickly before the animal weakens to the point that it cannot survive surgery and anesthesia.

Uterine Inertia

When the muscles of the uterus no longer will or can contract to push out the kits, the problem is called uterine inertia. This condition requires immediate emergency care. Your veterinarian will decide if oxytocin injections may be helpful to stimulate the weak muscles of the uterus to contract. In some cases, oxytocin is not effective or may be dangerous and a cesarean section is necessary.

Hemorrhage

The female's uterus can tear or rupture, or the vagina may tear, during prolonged or difficult birth. Signs of uterine hemorrhage (excessive bleeding) include vaginal bleeding and inability to deliver kits.

Hypocalcemia, Eclampsia, Puerperal Tetany

Hypocalcemia is a life-threatening condition caused by low blood levels of calcium, or a calcium deficiency. It is usually seen during lactation when the female is nursing her kits. It can also occur during pregnancy.

Symptoms include depression and muscle spasms. If emergency treatment (an injection of calcium gluconate) is not given immediately, convulsions and death follow rapidly.

Failure to Lactate

It is very important for kits to receive colostrum, the "milk" produced in the first hours after birth. Colostrum contains substances that protect the kits against some diseases while they are growing. Some females fail to produce colostrum or milk (agalactia), or cannot produce enough milk to feed their babies adequately. Kits that do not have enough to eat are weak and thin.

Milk letdown may take a while but should start at least 12 hours after giving birth. If your chinchilla's kits seem like they are constantly hungry or if they are vocalizing often and not gaining weight, contact your veterinarian. An injection of oxytocin, a substance that stimulates lactation, may help. If your chinchilla is not able to feed her kits, you will have to hand-feed them.

Hair Rings (Fur Rings)

Male chinchillas should be checked regularly for hair rings. These are strands of hair that become tightly twisted around the penis, causing swelling, pain, tissue death, and the inability to retract the penis back completely into its sheath

Good homes should be lined up for your kits before you breed your chinchillas.

(paraphimosis). Hair rings are observed most often after mating but can occur at any time. Hair rings may be so tight that they prevent urination. If not removed, they may lead to loss of the penis or death.

Hair rings can be removed by gently lubricating the penis (use K-Y Jelly, Priority Care, or mineral oil) and slipping the hair off the penis; or by carefully cutting the hair away with fine scissors. If the penis is extremely swollen, contact your veterinarian immediately.

By now you have gained a lot of knowledge about chinchillas. You know hard work is needed to keep your chinchillas healthy during the breeding season and during those delicate and vulnerable first stages of life. As a serious, dedicated chinchilla breeder, you have your work cut out for you! Good luck and have fun!

Chapter Ten
The Chinchilla Connoisseur

Every chinchilla is unique. Each has its own delightful personality. The icing on the cake, though, is the chinchilla's glorious coat and the variety of beautiful colors that breeders can produce. When breeders have top-quality animals, they put them to the test by exhibiting them in chinchilla shows.

Chinchilla shows are a lot of fun. They are also a great place to meet interesting people, learn, gain experience, and purchase a beautiful chinchilla for your breeding program or for show. (Breeder listings and show information can be obtained from the Empress Chinchilla Breeders Cooperative and the Mutation Chinchilla Breeders Association web sites, see "Useful Addresses and Literature.")

It takes an eye for beauty, an understanding of genetics, knowledge of the standards of quality, and a lot of study and enthusiasm to make the leap from chinchilla hobbyist to chinchilla connoisseur. So are you ready to take the challenge and test yourself and your chinchillas to

The standard blue gray, or "naturelle," usually has an agouti coat pattern.

see how things measure up? If so, it is time to check out the show scene!

Know Your Colors

Chinchillas come in a lot of different colors. Show classes are grouped by the animals' sex, age, and color. Genetics and coat color inheritance in chinchillas are very complicated subjects that are outside the scope of this handbook but covered in depth in the literature (see "Useful Addresses and Literature"). To be successful in producing beautiful coat colors, the breeder must have a firm understanding of basic genetic principles, excellent breeding and show stock, an overwhelming desire to succeed, and a lot of patience, skill, and luck!

The descriptions and classifications of chinchillas vary according to breeders, clubs, associations, and countries. So in order to truly know your colors, you must see them in real life by attending shows, visiting chinchilla breeders, and studying the definitions. If you plan on showing your chinchillas, be sure to get a

The mosaic chinchilla is a blend of white and other colors, such as blue, black, or beige.

copy of the rules, standards, and definition of acceptable colors of the association hosting the show *before* you enter your animals. This will ensure that you enter them in the correct color classes, according to the club's or organization's terminology. Remember, not all colors are defined and described the same by different groups.

The following is a general description of some colors found in chinchillas.

Standard blue gray, also called naturelle: This color is referred to as the standard color. Other color variations are usually referred to as mutations. The standard blue gray is a beautiful silvery blue gray that comes in a variety of shades. The standard is usually also agouti, having a wild-type pattern. Agouti pigmentation is named after the agouti, a wild South American rodent. Agouti coloration is observed in many species of animals

(rabbits, squirrels) and is characterized by individual hair shafts having alternate dark and light bands of color. Agouti patterns help camouflage prey animals from predators in their environment. For example, agouti blue gray chinchillas would blend in well on volcanic rocks in their natural surroundings.

The standard blue gray chinchilla has slate blue fur extending a long distance up from the bottom of the hair shaft. This band is called the undercolor. Although it appears slate, it is really a dilute black. When progressing up the hair shaft, the next color encountered is white. This is called the bar. Finally, the tip of the hair is black, and this is called veiling or ticking. Veiling is most concentrated, or dark, on the animal's back, lightens down the sides of the body, and disappears at the belly. As a result, the belly is white, yellow-white, or cream white.

White: There are a lot of variations of white chinchillas. A white chinchilla should be a very clean white, without a yellow tinge or other hues. White chinchillas may have dark eyes and dark or beige guard hairs, or they may have a mosaic or broken pattern of other colors mixed in the white fur. Or, a white chinchilla may be a true albino with pink eyes. Some white chinchillas are referred to as stone whites. These carry a gene that, when expressed in the homozygous form, cause anophthalmia (absence of eyes) or microphthalmia (smaller-than-normal eyes). This same type of disorder has been associated with a white gene in other species, such as dwarf hamsters.

Black velvet chinchillas are a deep, dark, black. They have white bellies and black eyes.

Ebony and charcoal: These chinchillas are black in color and have a white belly and black eyes.

Sapphire chinchillas are a metallic blue in color and can range in shades from light to dark. The belly is white.

Violet chinchillas are lighter in color than sapphires and have a lavendar cast to their fur, similar to a blue-point Siamese cat. The body is a light color, and the face, feet, and tail are pigmented violet. The color ranges in shades from light to very dark.

Beige: This color is well described by its name. The belly is white. Beige chinchillas vary in shades from a light champagne to dark beige. They have pink, dark, ruby red or black eyes.

Mosaics are a blend of white and other colors, such as blue, black, or beige. They may appear to be a white body with colored patches or a dark body color with white patches.

Miscellany: These are colors that do not fit any of the above descriptions.

There are many types of white chinchillas. This pink-white chinchilla has some pigmentation in its fur. Its dark eyes add to its beauty.

Genetics of Coat Color Inheritance

Coat color inheritance is complicated. However, if you have a passion for genetics, this just might be the subject for you! Detailed explanations of genetics and coat color inheritance are available in numerous books. An excellent guide that deals specifically with the chinchilla is published by the Mutation Chinchilla Breeders Association of the Empress Chinchilla Breeders Cooperative entitled *Basic Genetics of the Coat Color of Chinchilla*. This is a must-have for the serious breeder who aspires to be an expert on coat color. With careful planning, excellent breeding records, and a good knowledge of color inheritance, who knows? You just might produce the next beautiful color mutation. Study hard and good luck!

Reserving a Chinchilla for Show and Breeding

You would think that it would be easy to find exactly what you want for breeding and exhibition when you want it. The truth is, though, many

Black velvet chinchillas are very popular. Their light colored undersides contrast sharply with their deep black coat color.

Here are some things you can do to maximize your chances of success:

• Make sure you have the time, space, and money for your hobby before you begin.

• Invest in the best. Start with the best animal stock you can afford.

• Give your animals the best food and housing possible.

• Find an experienced breeder to be your mentor.

• Continue to learn as much as you can about chinchillas.

• Be patient.

• Know how to recognize animals you should cull.

• Keep your animal facility very clean.

• Keep accurate breeding records.

• Keep accurate health records.

• Join your local and national chinchilla clubs, and be an active participant.

• Most of all, have fun!

qualities are inherited in a recessive manner and are not produced often or in large numbers. It may take quite a while before a breeder can offer you a chinchilla that comes close to your specifications. You may have to settle for something slightly different than what you had planned on or be very, very patient until just the right chin comes along.

Be sure to buy the best animals you can from established, reputable breeders that are willing to part with quality animals in their herd. There is a lot to learn to be successful at this challenging hobby, and you will be starting from scratch. You will need the help and guidance of experienced breeders as you begin your hobby and continue throughout the years.

Traveling with Your Chinchilla

If you are going to participate in shows, you will be doing a lot of traveling and so will your chins. Traveling with your pet is easy if you keep these few things in mind:

1. Never travel with your chinchilla, or expose it to other animals, if it is sick or if it has recently been exposed to sick animals.

2. Never leave your chinchilla in a vehicle on a warm day, even if you are parked in the shade and the windows are open.

This dark ebony chinchilla is in beautiful condition and ready for the show table.

3. Use a small cat flight kennel, wire carrier, or small cage designed for travel. Cover it with a light cloth to help block out bright light and loud sounds, but do not block ventilation. Fresh air is important!

4. Place an absorbent towel on the floor of the travel kennel.

5. Place a hideaway in the travel kennel.

6. Give your pet a small piece of fruit for moisture during transport.

7. Give your pet some loose hay or hay cubes for food.

8. If you are traveling by car, make sure the travel kennel is positioned so that it cannot flip, fall, or be jostled. It should be fastened in with a seatbelt when possible.

9. If you are traveling by air, the airlines will require advanced reservations for you to be able to keep your pet with you in the cabin (limit is two pets per cabin). Make sure your travel kennel is small enough to fit under the seat in front of you.

10. If you are traveling by air or out of state, you will need a veterinary health certificate dated within ten days of travel. A certificate of acclimation may also be required by the airlines.

Things to Pack for Your Pet's Trip

• Commercial bottled water
• Water bottle and sipper tube (if the trip is more than a few hours long)
• Hay cubes and a piece of fruit

• Grooming supplies (combs, brush, dust bath)
• Absorbent cloth towels, large and small
• Bag for trash
• Paper towels
• Hand wipes (for you)

You Be the Judge!

Chinchillas are usually judged in groups of ten. Animals are exhibited on a table. A chinchilla must be at least four months old to compete in a show. Age classes are usually divided into two groups, animals seven months and older and animals younger than seven months of age. Males compete against males, and females compete against females.

Classes are also divided by colors. Competitors (also called entrants) can exhibit a maximum of 20 animals in a color class, although most individuals do not have that many animals of the same color to show at one time.

Judges make their selections according to body type, coat color,

This brown velvet chinchilla has freckled ears!

and coat density. A large, robust chinchilla is more desirable than a slender, gangly chinchilla. The coat color is judged on several aspects, including clarity, lack of red or yellow tints (undesirable), and veiling (how well and how completely the most deeply pigmented color of the coat covers the body). Coat density is very important to judges. The ideal coat is thick and plush. By considering all the qualities of all the animals in a class and

comparing them with each other, the judge makes a decision. A judge can award more than one first place if more than one animal is deserving of the award. If no animals deserve first place, the judge can withhold the award and give out second and third place prizes. If the class is not a good one, the judge can decide not to give out any awards at all. Naturally, not everyone agrees with every judge. However, it is important to be a good sport and follow the old but wise advice, "Win without boasting, lose without excuses."

No matter what the judge decides, you are the real judge. After all, you make important judgments concerning your chinchillas every day, about housing, food, and care. You decide which chinchillas to buy, which ones to breed, which ones to keep, and which ones to sell. You select the ones that you think are the best, and you cull the ones that do not meet your standards. You set your standards. If you raise the bar high in that regard, you will evaluate your animals more critically than any judge ever would. Also, you have the benefit of having more information and knowing more about your chinchillas than the judge. After all, the judge does not know your pets' pedigree, breeding history, or medical records—but you do! In addition to their appearance, you also know if your animals are good breeders, good parents, and free of genetic or health problems that might not be obvious at a show. If you

Homozygous beige is arguably one of the most beautifully colored chinchillas.

Violet chinchillas have a lavender hue to their fur. Coloration can range from light to dark.

are a good chinchilla breeder, based on what you see and what you know about your chinchillas, you already know which ones are truly worthy of an award. Of course, a lot depends not only on the judge but on the competition that day. The judge is there to confirm that you are on the right track. In the end, though, you are the ultimate judge of your own animals!

Chinchilla shows should be a place to meet interesting people, see beautiful animals, and learn and have fun. If that is what you do at a chinchilla show, then you have already won!

The Magic Continues

With the wide range of chinchilla personalities and colors, picking a favorite is hard! Like so many other chinchilla lovers, you may feel the temptation to start an entire collection. You may wonder if a magical spell has come over you and you

have become enchanted with chins. If so, join the crowd! It is not unusual to hear chinchilla fanciers exclaim, "You can never have too many!" Of course, everything has its limits, but it is fun to dream and scheme.

The chinchilla has proven itself to be a wonderful, beautiful, fascinating companion. From the Andes mountains of Chile to the shores of faraway lands, from the brink of extinction to fur farms and research laboratories, and from the show table straight into your loving home—the chinchilla is a survivor and a true gem of nature. It has come a long way from the volcanic rock crevices it inhabited for millennia. Some of the mysteries of its fascinating history have been solved, but most remain secrets. The chinchilla is a charming enigma and an adored pet.

So prepare to be enchanted. Take some time out and snuggle down with your chinchilla. Feel its plush coat, look into its bright eyes, and enjoy the magic of the moment!

Useful Addresses and Literature

Organizations

American Association of Zoo
Veterinarians
6 North Pennell Road
Media, PA 19063
(610) 892-4812
www.aazv.org

American Society of Mammologists
P.O. Box 7060
Lawrence, KS 66044
(785) 843-1235
(800) 627-0629
www.mammalsociety.org

American Veterinary Medical
Association
1931 N. Meacham Road
Suite 100
Schaumberg, IL 60173-4360
(847) 925-8070
www.avma.org

Empress Chinchilla Breeders
Cooperative
P.O. Box 318
Sixes, OR 97476
www.harborside.com

Mutation Chinchilla Breeders
Association
1228 Red Hill Road
Pennsburg, PA 18073
www.mutationchinchillas.com

Recommended Reading

Anderson, S., Jones, J. K., eds.
Orders and Families of Recent Mammals of the World. New York, NY: Wiley, 1984.

Bowen, E. G., Jenkins, R. W. *Chinchilla History, Husbandry, Marketing.* Hackensack, NJ: Alder Printing Co., 1969.

Donnelly, T. M., Quimby, F. W. *Chinchillas: Biology of Laboratory Animals.* Orlando, FL: Academic Press, 1974.

Guttman, H. N. *Guidelines for the Well-Being of Rodents in Research.* Research Triangle Park: Scientists Center for Animal Welfare, 1990.

Hillyer, E. V., Quesenberry, K. E., Donnelly, T. M. *Ferrets, Rabbits, and Rodents: Chapter 23: Biology and Husbandry of Chinchillas.* Philadelphia, PA: W. B. Saunders Company, 1997.

Give your chinchilla lots of tender loving care and it will give you many years of friendship and fun in return.

Houston, J. W., Prestwich, J. P. *Chinchilla Care*. Los Angeles, CA: Borden Publishing Company, 1962.

Kraft, H. *Diseases of Chinchillas.* Neptune City, NJ: T.F.H. Publications, 1987.

Laber-Laird, K., Swindle, M. M., Flecknell, P. *Handbook of Rodent and Rabbit Medicine*. New York, NY: Elsevier Science, 1996.

Mutation Chinchilla Breeders Association of the Empress Chinchilla Breeders Cooperative, Inc. *Basic Genetics of the Coat Color of Chinchilla*. 1970.

Nowak, R. M., ed. *Walker's Mammals of the World*, 5th edition, Volume II. Baltimore, MD: The Johns Hopkins University Press, 1991.

Parker, W. D. *Modern Chinchilla Fur Farming*. Alhambra, CA: Borden Publishing Co., 1975.

Rowlands, I. W., Weir, B. J., eds. *The Biology of Hystricomorph Rodents (The Proceedings of a Symposium Held at the Zoological Society of London)*. Published for The Zoological Society of London by Academic Press, 1974.

Searle, A. G. *Comparative Genetics of Coat Colour in Mammals*. London, UK: Logos Press Limited, 1967.

Spotorno, A. E., Zuleta, C. A., Valladares, J. P., Deane, A. L., Jiménez, J. E. *"Chinchilla laniger," Mammalian Species,* no. 758, pp. 1–9, December 2004.

Index

If you have several chinchillas in your breeding colony, make sure there are enough chew toys for everyone to share.